# SUCH A CLASH OF ARMS

C CASEMATE | ILLUSTRATED

# SUCH A CLASH OF ARMS

## The Maryland Campaign, September 1862

Kevin R. Pawlak

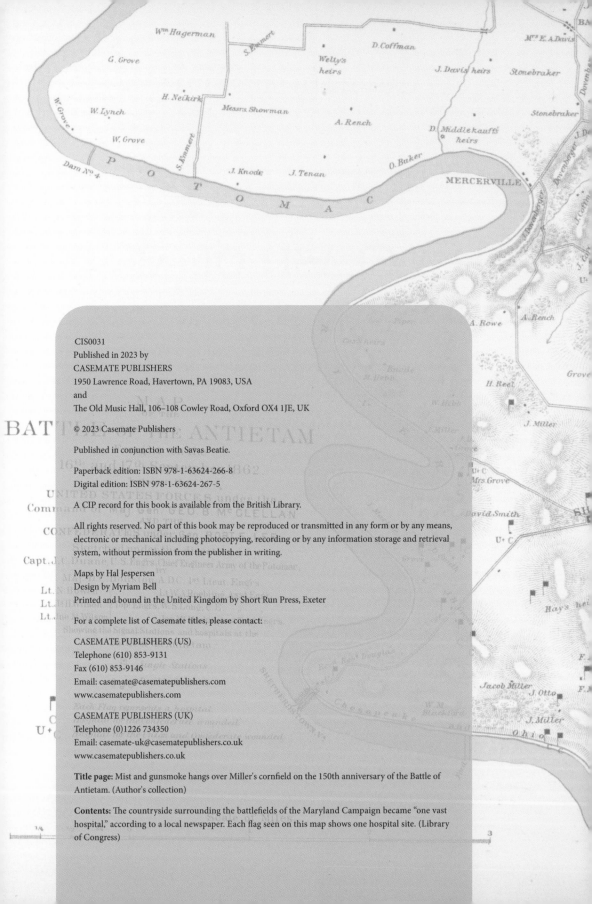

CIS0031

Published in 2023 by
CASEMATE PUBLISHERS
1950 Lawrence Road, Havertown, PA 19083, USA
and
The Old Music Hall, 106–108 Cowley Road, Oxford OX4 1JE, UK

Published in conjunction with Savas Beatie.

Paperback edition: ISBN 978-1-63624-266-8
Digital edition: ISBN 978-1-63624-267-5

A CIP record for this book is available from the British Library.

Maps by Hal Jespersen
Design by Myriam Bell
Printed and bound in the United Kingdom by Short Run Press, Exeter

For a complete list of Casemate titles, please contact:

CASEMATE PUBLISHERS (US)
Telephone (610) 853-9131
Fax (610) 853-9146
Email: casemate@casematepublishers.com
www.casematepublishers.com

CASEMATE PUBLISHERS (UK)
Telephone (0)1226 734350
Email: casemate-uk@casematepublishers.co.uk
www.casematepublishers.co.uk

**Title page:** Mist and gunsmoke hangs over Miller's cornfield on the 150th anniversary of the Battle of Antietam. (Author's collection)

**Contents:** The countryside surrounding the battlefields of the Maryland Campaign became "one vast hospital," according to a local newspaper. Each flag seen on this map shows one hospital site. (Library of Congress)

# Contents

# | Timeline

**July 22, 1862** — Abraham Lincoln shows his Cabinet a draft of the Preliminary Emancipation Proclamation. Secretary of State William Seward convinces him to wait for a victory before announcing it to the country.

**August 30** — Confederate victory at battle of Second Manassas.

**September 2** — Major General George B. McClellan assumes command of Union forces in Washington, DC.

**September 4–6** — General Robert E. Lee's Army of Northern Virginia crosses the Potomac River into Maryland.

**September 7** — McClellan leaves Washington and makes his headquarters in the field with the Army of the Potomac.

**September 8** — Lee issues a proclamation to the people of Maryland.

**September 9** — Lee issues Special Orders No. 191.

**September 12** — Major General "Stonewall" Jackson's forces capture Martinsburg, Virginia. Skirmishing begins atop Maryland Heights. The vanguard of the Army of the Potomac enters Frederick.

**September 13** — Battle of Maryland Heights. McClellan and the Army of the Potomac enters Frederick. The Lost Orders found and delivered to McClellan.

**September 14** — Battle of South Mountain. Confederates converge on Harpers Ferry.

**September 15** — Surrender of Harpers Ferry.

**September 16** — Armies gather on the banks of Antietam Creek outside Sharpsburg, Maryland.

**September 17** — Battle of Antietam.

| September 18 | Lee moves into Virginia. |
| September 19–20 | Battle of Shepherdstown. The Maryland Campaign ends. |
| September 22 | Lincoln announces the Preliminary Emancipation Proclamation. |

▲ An unidentified Confederate soldier lies on the battlefield awaiting burial. (Library of Congress)

# Introduction

Since the start of the American Civil War, the Potomac River carved out the Confederacy's northern border. Up to this point in the war, no major Confederate force had crossed it. Much of the fighting in the Eastern Theater had been well south of it in Virginia. Beginning on September 4, 1862, and lasting over the next three days, victorious, exuberant Confederate troops splashed into its cold waters and dried their feet on its north shore. This was Maryland soil, and now Confederate feet trod on it by the thousands.

▼ Major General John Pope was known for his combative nature and self-confidence. He initiated a new way of fighting the Civil War by waging "hard war." Disliked by many officers in the Army of the Potomac, Pope's stint in the war's Eastern Theater was brief and ended following the battle of Second Manassas. (Library of Congress)

Just a few months earlier, few citizens of both the United and Confederate States could have believed that gray-clad soldiers would reach the Potomac's banks. Then, Major General George B. McClellan's Army of the Potomac was not near its namesake river. Instead, it was wrapping itself around the Confederate capital of Richmond over 100 miles to the south. Some predicted that 1862's Fourth of July celebrations would not only commemorate the United States' independence, but also its reunification.

Then, in late June, General Robert E. Lee lashed out at McClellan with his Army of Northern Virginia, an army Lee had been in command of for less than one month. For nearly one week, the distant sounds of cannon and musketry echoed in Richmond's streets. During the Seven Days Campaign, Lee bullied the Federals away from his capital. There would be no celebrations of the country's reunification on July 4, 1862.

Both armies licked their wounds in the wake of the weeklong campaign. Back in Washington, DC, President Abraham

Lincoln undertook a new effort to add extra strength to the Northern war effort in the Eastern theater. From the West, he brought Major General John Pope to command the newly created Army of Virginia. Additionally, Lincoln appointed Major General Henry Halleck as General in Chief of the United States Army.

Pope and Halleck, driven by Lincoln and Secretary of War Edwin Stanton, brought quick changes to the Northern war effort.

Pope, a Republican, implemented harsh policies against Virginia civilians in the northern and central part of the state should they attempt to hinder Federal operations. Halleck received the task of reinvigorating the northern war machine that had so far failed to capture Richmond that summer.

Following a visit to the Army of the Potomac's camp at Harrison's Landing, Halleck determined the best course of action was to unite Pope's Army of Virginia

▶ Lee's victory at the battle of Second Manassas was his greatest, and served as a springboard for his army to cross the Potomac River. This monument commemorates the lives of the Union soldiers lost in the battle. (Author's collection)

◄ Frustrated by the course of the war in the east, President Abraham Lincoln constantly found McClellan to be untrustworthy and openly defiant of the administration. That July, Lincoln sought to change the scope and goals of the war by issuing a proclamation freeing enslaved people in the southern states. He felt he first needed a military victory to issue the proclamation, though. (Library of Congress)

and McClellan's army north of Richmond. Once combined, these two armies would overwhelmingly outnumber Lee's Confederates and present a serious threat to the Confederate capital.

Once Lee confirmed McClellan's departure from the Peninsula, he shifted his army north of the city to face Pope and defeat him before the two Federal armies united. Initially, Pope thwarted Lee's designs. Time favored the Federals. By mid-August, the Army of the Potomac was leaving the Peninsula and arriving in northern Virginia to link with the Army of Virginia. On August 25, Lee sent Major General Thomas "Stonewall" Jackson on a sweeping move around Pope's army. The next day, Jackson's men severed the Federal supply line, forcing Pope back towards Washington. From August 28 to 30, 1862, Union and Confederate forces converged and fought on the old Bull Run battlefield, the scene of the war's first major battle 13 months earlier.

On August 29, Pope, unaware of the reunification of Jackson's men with the other half of Lee's army under Major General James Longstreet, attacked Jackson's line but failed to break it. Pope ordered a larger attack the next day that also was futile. Lee and Longstreet followed up its repulse with a counterattack that swept Pope's army from the field. In three days of fighting, the battle of Second Manassas produced approximately 22,000 casualties.

By the summer of 1862, Lincoln decided to raise the stakes of the war. On July 22, 1862, he announced to his Cabinet his intention to issue a preliminary emancipation proclamation that would free slaves in the Confederacy. Lincoln's mind was made up on the matter, though he did solicit his Cabinet's advice. Secretary of State William Seward offered an important insight: issuing such a sweeping proclamation while the Union war effort produced no major victories would appear to be a "last *shriek* on the retreat," he said. Seward urged Lincoln to hold the proclamation's announcement "until you can give it to the country supported by military success." The President concurred. Lincoln waited for that victory for the remainder of July and all of August, but no victory came. Instead, a defeated Union army limped back into the defenses of Washington while Lee's army was poised to exploit its success north of the Potomac River in Maryland and Pennsylvania.

# The Campaign Begins

Ninety days after he assumed command of the Army of Northern Virginia, Gen. Robert E. Lee took the war from the gates of Richmond to the outskirts of Washington. North of the Potomac River, Lee sought another victory that would achieve many objectives for the Confederacy, namely its independence. While Lee's men crossed into Maryland, President Lincoln turned to Maj. Gen. George B. McClellan to drive the Confederates back into Virginia.

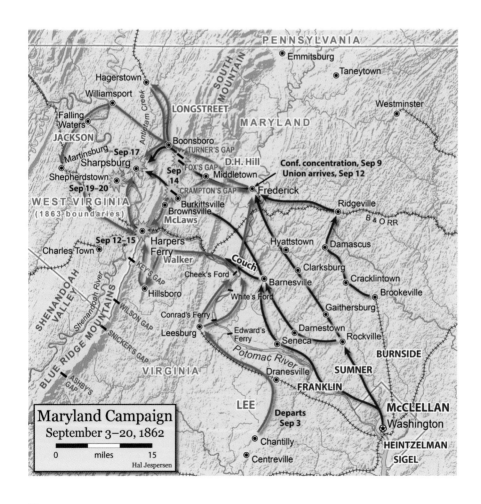

Maryland Campaign
September 3–20, 1862

0    miles    15

Hal Jespersen

▲ Thousands of Confederates crossed the Potomac River fords near Leesburg. The crossing was well documented by many Confederates, who knew it was a momentous occasion. (Library of Congress)

Moments before splashing into the Potomac River near Leesburg, Virginia, Colonel John B. Gordon of the 6th Alabama Infantry halted his men on the Old Dominion's shore. Gordon wanted them to know the importance of the occasion. The colonel compared his men's plunging into the Potomac to Washington's crossing of the Delaware River. "Future generations should rise up and call us blessed," he proclaimed before ordering his troops into the water, the temperature of which "decidedly dampened" their fervor. Regardless, the joy of entering Maryland could not be restrained within the Army of Northern Virginia's ranks. "Men stopped midway in the stream and sang loudly," wrote one South Carolinian. "Never before had an occurrence so excited and enlivened the spirits of the troops as the crossing of

the Potomac into the land of our sister, Maryland."

Following the conclusion of the Second Manassas Campaign on September 1, 1862, Robert E. Lee eyed Maryland and Pennsylvania beyond as his next theater of operations. "The present seems to be the most propitious time since the commencement of the war for the Confederate Army to enter Maryland," Lee wrote President Jefferson Davis on September 3, 1862. The general understood time was of the essence. He knew he could not assault the Union army while it was behind Washington's strong fortifications. And while he waited, new Federal recruits were pouring into the Union capital. When ready, their strength would further tip the numerical scales in the Union's favor. While his army was not in the best shape following

# Profile: General Robert E. Lee, 1807–70

Born to a hero of the American Revolution—Henry "Light-Horse Harry" Lee—on January 19, 1807, Robert E. Lee's own military career began when he graduated second in the United States Military Academy's Class of 1829. Lee served as an engineer across the growing United States. During the country's war with Mexico, Captain Lee served on Gen. Winfield Scott's staff during the American march on Mexico City. Scott grew fond of Lee, who earned three brevet promotions for his service. Lee continued engineering stints after the conflict ended and served as West Point's superintendent. He led a force of United States Marines in the capture of John Brown at Harpers Ferry on October 18, 1859. At the beginning of the Civil War, Scott offered Lee command of United States forces. Lee turned Scott down and resigned from the United States Army before offering his services to his native state, Virginia, and ultimately to the Confederacy. Lee prepared Virginia for war in the early months of the conflict. In the fall of 1861, he unsuccessfully led Confederate forces in western Virginia. That winter, he examined Confederate fortifications along the Atlantic coast before returning to Richmond for the spring campaign to serve as President Jefferson Davis' military advisor. In this capacity, Lee devised "Stonewall" Jackson's 1862 Shenandoah Valley Campaign. Major General Joseph Johnston's wounding outside of Richmond pushed Lee into command of the Army of Northern Virginia, which he led for the rest of the war. He drove Union forces away from Richmond in the summer of 1862 and moved his army north to relieve Virginians from the war and try to achieve a war-winning victory in Maryland, something he constantly sought but failed to do. Lee's battlefield triumphs in 1862–63 made him and his army the idols of the Confederacy. However, Lee could not continue his victorious streak later in 1863 and throughout 1864–65 and surrendered his army at Appomattox Courthouse on April 9, 1865. Lee humbly assumed the presidency of Washington College after the war. He died on October 12, 1870.

▼ Robert E. Lee. (Library of Congress)

the marching and fighting of the Seven Days and Second Manassas campaigns, Maryland still beckoned to Lee. "Still we cannot afford to be idle, and though weaker than our opponents in men and military equipments, must endeavor to harass, if we cannot destroy them."

A Confederate movement into Maryland had the potential to provide the Confederacy multiple political, diplomatic, and military advantages. Since 1861, enticing Maryland to leave the Union was a goal of the nascent Confederate government. That border state—one that permitted slavery but did not secede—surrounded Washington, DC, held important water and rail transportation routes, and was home to Baltimore, one of the nation's largest cities. Great Britain and France monitored the Confederacy's progress in the Eastern Theater and a victory on Northern soil might bring formal recognition of the new nation with a victory on Northern soil.

Lee's army could live off the Maryland countryside and provide Virginia farmers with a respite from tramping armies. Additionally, Southern troops north of the Potomac River could swing votes in the upcoming fall elections in the North in favor of a peace movement.

All of these considerations and perhaps more weighed on Lee's mind as he ordered his army across the Potomac River. However, one consideration outweighed all the others. "I went into Maryland to give battle," Lee said after the war. A battle—and not just any battle, but another Confederate victory—could reap huge benefits for the Confederacy, including all the considerations mentioned above. Lee sought battlefield success over the Army of the Potomac more than anything else.

From September 4 to 7, 1862, Lee's battle-hardened soldiers waded the shallow Potomac waters and marched to Frederick. There, they settled into camps

▼ The Virginia State Capitol in Richmond was designed by Thomas Jefferson and completed in 1788. By July 1861, the Virginia General Assembly began to share the building with the Confederate Congress. The building became a symbol of the Confederacy and southern defiance. Here, decisions were made that shaped the Confederacy's war effort and objectives. (Library of Congress)

along the city's east side near the waters of the Monocacy River preparing for the next phase of the campaign.

Approximately 40 miles to the southeast, the Lincoln administration dealt with the fallout of the defeat at Second Manassas. Major General John Pope, the beaten commander on that battlefield, could not be retained in command. "This was our great disaster and had the effect to greatly demoralize our whole army. Men lost confidence in their generals," said an Ohio soldier. They especially lost confidence in Pope. President Lincoln felt he had no other man to turn to than Maj. Gen. George B. McClellan.

It was not an easy decision. The spring and summer campaigns had tested the relationship between the commander-in-chief, his advisors, and the 35-year-old

general. Despite cabinet member threats to resign if McClellan should be appointed in command of the Union troops around Washington, Lincoln felt he had no choice, though he did query others who turned down the command offer. To his secretary John Hay, Lincoln said of McClellan, "we must use what tools we have. There is no man in the army who can man these fortifications and lick these troops of ours into shape half as well as he." Then, the president concluded, "But he is too useful just now to sacrifice."

On September 2, Lincoln and General-in-Chief Henry Halleck appointed McClellan as the commander of Washington's forces. Clustered behind the powerful earthworks ringing the city were McClellan's Army of the Potomac, Pope's Army of Virginia, troops from western Virginia and the

▼ One of the larger homes in Leesburg in 1862, Harrison Hall offered a welcome reprieve for Lee and his staff. Next door still sits the home of doctor Samuel Jackson who worked on Lee's injured arms. Lee met with his principal subordinates here on September 5, 1862, to discuss the army's movement into Maryland. Of all the events that took place here in September 1862, the most important to Lee was probably seeing his son, Robert Lee, Jr., on a short visit. (Author's collection)

## Army Experience

Though both armies had plenty of hardened veterans in their ranks during the Maryland Campaign, the Army of the Potomac carried a recent influx of newly enlisted soldiers. This group comprised nearly one-quarter of the army's infantry. Additionally, only 10 percent of the Federals had been in three or more major battles prior to the campaign. Comparatively, over 60 percent of Confederate soldiers had the experience of being in three or more major battles before marching into Maryland.

Carolinas, and thousands of recently raised recruits who had yet to feel the fatigue of a long march or the adrenaline of battle. The emergency of the moment required quick work. As early as September 4, Federal soldiers were moving through the city on their way to Maryland. Two days later, McClellan cobbled together the Union forces into one as newly reconstituted Army of the Potomac. On September 7, Lincoln and Halleck visited the general at his house in Washington. "General, you will take command of the forces in the field," Lincoln said. McClellan departed for his army's positions in Maryland that night.

Despite McClellan's restoration to command and the morale boost it gave the Army of the Potomac—many loved the man they called "Little Mac"—Union soldiers felt drained by the repeated losses. "As for the future I have no hopes whatever," wrote Federal staff officer Washington Roebling. "I assure you on Saturday night last [August 30] I felt utterly sick, disgusted and tired of the war; being somewhat rested now, I feel more hopeful." But even sleep could not fully restore Roebling's optimism. "Our men are sick of the war; they fight without an aim and without enthusiasm." Another soldier

wrote, "The advent of McClellan restored confidence, but the situation was still alarming." Soldiers of both armies knew the stakes of the coming campaign in Maryland.

McClellan embarked on the campaign north of the Potomac guided by three principal objectives. First, his movement northwest from the capital had to protect Washington and Baltimore. Then, McClellan had to ensure the enemy did not invade Pennsylvania. Lastly, Lincoln tasked McClellan with driving the enemy out of Maryland and back into Virginia. Lincoln and McClellan both felt the necessity of meeting Lee in Maryland and expelling him from the state. McClellan believed the state of his army was far from ideal and that once his objectives were completed, "so much remained to be done to place the army in condition" for the next campaign that he needed time to reinvigorate the Army of the Potomac. But first, he needed to get Lee out of Maryland.

To achieve these multiple objectives, the army commander divided his 60,000 men and over 300 guns into three parts. Major General Ambrose Burnside commanded the army's right wing, composed of Joseph Hooker's First Corps and Jesse Reno's Ninth Corps. In the center, the army's oldest general, Edwin Sumner, directed his own Second Corps and Brigadier General Alpheus Williams's Twelfth Corps as well as the army's division of United States Regulars under Brigadier General George Sykes. Major General William Franklin's Sixth Corps, augmented by a division of the Fourth Corps, constituted the army's reserve.

From above, the Army of the Potomac would have appeared as a three-pronged fork coming out of Washington and headed northwest towards Frederick, Maryland. The bulk of the army, McClellan's center, concentrated around Rockville and formed into battle line behind Muddy Branch to protect Washington. Franklin's reserve on the army's left guarded the fords of the Potomac River in the rear of Seneca Creek. These two prongs essentially marked time for a few days to protect Washington and gather intelligence about the enemy's position and intentions. Additionally, McClellan and his subordinates used this time "to place the army in fair condition." While the center and left shielded Washington from enemy forces in Frederick—the two cities are only 40 miles apart—Burnside's right wing marched north to protect Baltimore.

That was the tallest task early in the campaign. Burnside's two corps headed towards the National Road, the macadamized artery connecting Baltimore to Frederick, approximately 50 miles apart, and beyond to the Ohio River. McClellan felt confident enough about the movement of Burnside's wing that by the evening of September 8, he informed Halleck, "I think that we are now in position to prevent any attack in force on Baltimore, while we cover Washington on this side." McClellan ordered an advance of the entire army the next day.

Brigadier General Alfred Pleasonton's cavalry patrolled in front of the Federal main body to screen the army's movements and to gather information about the enemy. Several small but severe cavalry clashes occurred during this time, first at Poolesville on September 5 and again at Poolesville, Beallsville, and Barnesville on September 8–9. The blue-clad horsemen came out on top in each of the desperate fights. Despite the gains, Confederate troops still clung to Sugarloaf Mountain between Barnesville and Frederick. Control of the mountain would grant either army an extensive view of the surrounding countryside and of their opposition's whereabouts, information that still remained elusive to both army commanders.

▼ The Beall-Dawson House in Rockville dates from 1815 and has hosted prominent visitors throughout its history, including—supposedly—the Marquis de Lafayette during his tour of the United States in 1824. McClellan used the house as his first headquarters in the field during the Maryland campaign. Today, the Montgomery County Historical Society operates it as a house museum. (Author's collection)

While the Army of the Potomac received a mostly warm reception from Maryland's residents, Robert E. Lee's Confederates were greeted in more mixed tones. Rumors of Confederate troops in the state pushed Frederick's citizens into "the greatest trepidation," wrote Dr. Lewis Steiner, a United States Sanitary Commission inspector in the city at the start of the campaign. "Invasion by the Southern army was considered equivalent to destruction," he continued. Some Frederick families fled the city for Pennsylvania rather than live under the Confederate army.

This was not what Lee expected. Many in the South believed Marylanders wanted to secede, that only Northern oppression was keeping them in the Union. Moving into Maryland would not only provide Virginia farmers with a respite from the army while it lived off the rich farmland of central and western Maryland, but might also add a new star to the Confederacy's banner. However, this proved troublesome. As Lee tried to charm Marylanders to support the Confederate cause, taking goods from the state's citizens would only engender loathing, not support, for his army.

On September 8, Lee issued a proclamation to Marylanders that expressed his intentions and tried to soothe their worries. "It is right that you should know

▶ Alfred Pleasonton's performance during the Peninsula Campaign caught the eye of George B. McClellan and earned him command of the Army of the Potomac's cavalry division during the Maryland Campaign. (Library of Congress)

the purpose that has brought the army under my command within the limits of your State, so far as that purpose concerning yourselves," Lee began. The general listed Marylanders' perceived grievances against the Federal government before offering them the aid of the Confederacy: "the people of the South have long wished to aid you in throwing off this foreign yoke, to enable you again to enjoy the inalienable rights of freemen, and restore independence and sovereignty to your State." This was the reason for Lee's entrance into the state, he said. Ultimately, the decision was theirs, not his. "It is for you to decide your destiny, freely and without constraint. This army will respect your choice whatever it may be, and while the Southern people will rejoice to welcome you to your natural position among them, they will only welcome you when you come of your own free will." With the exception of a couple hundred recruits, Marylanders did not join Lee's ranks.

While Lee moved his army into Maryland to make overtures to the state's people,

the movement across the Potomac River was also meant to send a message to the greater Northern population. Besides his September 8 proclamation to Marylanders, Lee also dictated a message to President Davis. Now was the time, Lee said, to suggest to the United States government that they recognize the Confederacy's independence. This would be done at a time "when it is in our power to inflict injury upon our adversary," the general continued. Always looking forward, he concluded, "The proposal of peace would enable the people of the United States to determine at their coming elections whether they will support those who favor a prolongation of the war, or those who wish to bring it to a termination," referring to the North's upcoming midterm elections.

Lee's calls to bring Maryland into the Confederacy and to begin talks declaring it an independent nation show the position of strength the seceded states occupied in the late summer of 1862. Lee's Army of Northern Virginia was not the only Confederate force moving north either.

▲ Today, one can drive to the crest of Sugarloaf Mountain and visit the site of the Federal signal station that was captured here on September 5. This view to the west is very similar to the view of 1862. (Author's collection)

If Lee hoped to convince Marylanders to throw off the yoke of the Lincoln administration and to persuade that same government of his nation's independence, he needed a victory north of the Potomac River. The general's decision to cross the river east of the Blue Ridge Mountains put him closer to Washington and Baltimore, feigning a threat to both cities. He knew that would bring the Union army out from behind Washington's defenses. Once Lee accomplished that, he planned to move west, "establish our communications with Richmond through the Valley of the Shenandoah, and, by threatening Pennsylvania, induce the enemy to follow" all while Lee's men moved closer to their supply line as the enemy's lengthened. Lee stressed after the war, too, the importance of keeping his line of supply and communication open through the Shenandoah Valley. "[I]n order to remain [in Maryland] for any time or to be in proper position for a battle when he chose or should be forced to deliver it," he said, he had to clear the valley.

The Shenandoah Valley provided Lee with a reliable, good road network that would bring him supplies—food, gunpowder, bullets, and shells—necessary to fight a battle, his main campaign objective. Thus, after resting his men in Frederick, Lee's sights turned away from central Maryland to two towns occupied by Union troops at the northern end of the Shenandoah Valley: Harpers Ferry and Martinsburg.

▲ Confederate President Jefferson Davis believed that a coordinated effort to invade the north could bring about peace and possibly foreign intervention on behalf of the Confederacy. Davis believed he had a good military mind and personally intervened often into the affairs of generals. (Library of Congress)

In western Virginia, William Loring led a force of 5,000 men towards Charleston. Kirby Smith and Braxton Bragg advanced their commands into Kentucky to try to coax that border state into joining the Confederacy. Further west, Sterling Price and Earl Van Dorn each led their respective armies to reclaim portions of northern Mississippi that fell to Union armies earlier in the year. The Confederacy was advancing across 1,000 miles of territory.

# One Army Splits, Another Converges

Once in Maryland, Robert E. Lee had hopes of remaining for some time and carrying the war further north. To do that, he first had to eliminate the Federal troops in the Shenandoah Valley. Lee divided his army to subdue those Union troops while Maj. Gen. George B. McClellan moved his reorganized Army of the Potomac towards Frederick.

Harpers Ferry always seemed destined for history. The town sat at the head of the Shenandoah Valley and at the convergence of the Potomac and Shenandoah rivers. By 1802, a Federal armory and arsenal were established there. The gun-making operations continued to grow; by the time of the Civil War, the factory had produced approximately 600,000 firearms. Abolitionist John Brown brought a force of Black and White men to the town in October 1859 to secure firearms and, he hoped, ignite a slave rebellion that would cripple slavery in the Southern states. It

◄ The best view of Harpers Ferry is from Maryland Heights. A strenuous but worthwhile hike leads you to a great perspective of the confluence of the Potomac and Shenandoah rivers. From this view, it is easy to understand why capturing Maryland Heights was critical for the Confederates. (Author's collection)

▲ The town of Harpers Ferry is not visible from Bolivar Heights because it sits in a valley between three mountains and two rivers. Maryland Heights (left) and Loudoun Heights (right) tower over the town. Camp Hill can be located by finding Anthony Hall—the armory superintendent's home before the war—the large brick building in the center of the image. (Author's collection)

failed. Virginia militia and United States Marines captured Brown and some of his force—they killed others while a few escaped—before trying Brown and finding him guilty on three counts. Virginia executed Brown on December 2, 1859. Brown's raid put the country another step closer to civil war.

The Civil War brought sudden and immense changes to Harpers Ferry. When Virginia seceded on April 17, 1861, the state's militia moved quickly to seize the armory and arsenal. But they found that United States soldiers had burned both. Militia and townspeople poked through the ashes to find what was left of the gunsmithing machinery and shipped it further south.

Besides the reasons for the town's rise to prominence, Harpers Ferry's location still made it an important location in the Civil War. Its position at the northern end of the Shenandoah Valley placed it in the way of marching Union armies trying to seize the valley as a back-door invasion route to Richmond while Confederate armies vied for its possession to secure a route that carried them close to Washington.

Additionally, two important east–west supply routes passed through and near the town: the Baltimore and Ohio Railroad and the Chesapeake and Ohio Canal. Another north–south-running railroad connected Harpers Ferry with Winchester 30 miles to the south.

Harpers Ferry itself sat in a bowl surrounded by three higher pieces of elevation. Maryland Heights towered 1,463 feet above sea level north of the town. The second largest height, Loudoun Heights, stood 1,180 feet south of Harpers Ferry. Two miles to the west, the smaller but still impressive Bolivar Heights (650 feet) ran north to south from the Potomac to the Shenandoah River. If properly defended, the surrounding heights protected the town and the important supply routes than ran through it. Lose them, though, and any defending force would have a hard time holding onto the town, the canal, and the railroad. Confederate general A. P. Hill recognized this when he said, "I would rather take the place twenty times than undertake to hold it once." In September 1862, the Union army tested that assessment.

To defend the Baltimore and Ohio Railroad, the Federal government established the Railroad Brigade in the spring of 1862 and headquartered it at Harpers Ferry. This unit's goal was to protect 380 miles of railroad from Confederate forays against it. The Railroad Brigade was not expected to fight any major armies, only Confederate guerrillas and cavalry raids harassing the tracks.

By September 1862, 58-year-old professional soldier Colonel Dixon Miles had been in command at Harpers Ferry for five months. The only serious threat he faced was in May 1862 during "Stonewall" Jackson's Shenandoah Valley Campaign, but then the high command in Washington dispatched Rufus Saxton to lead the defense of Harpers Ferry, which he successfully did. Miles's credentials were extensive but his most recent performance was questionable. He had been the subject of a court martial after First Manassas. His placement in Harpers Ferry, however, was due to the Federal government not wanting to shelve someone who had served in the army for 43 years. Putting him in Harpers Ferry kept him in the army but out of the way.

Confederate success in the summer of 1862 altered the situation in the Shenandoah Valley. On September 2, the 3,000-man Winchester garrison led by Brigadier General Julius White abandoned its post and withdrew to Harpers Ferry. The troops remained there with Miles

▼ A man much blamed for the disaster at Harpers Ferry, Col. Dixon Miles has been called incompetent, a fool, and a drunk. A native Marylander and a graduate of West Point in 1824, Miles served in several posts in the United States Army, including in the Mexican War and fighting Indians in the west. He commanded a division at the battle of First Bull Run but was in reserve near Centreville. He was accused of drunkenness and reassigned to protect the B & O Railroad in March 1862. (Library of Congress)

while White moved to Martinsburg to lead the 2,500 Federals there. Lee's movement into Maryland—a march Miles learned of quickly—further upset Federal plans in the Valley.

Once Lee's army crossed the Potomac River and converged at Frederick, it placed his army squarely between Miles's and White's garrisons and Washington and Baltimore. The Federals' decision to remain in the Shenandoah Valley derailed Lee's campaign plans. "It had been supposed that the advance upon Fredericktown would lead to the evacuation of Martinsburg and Harper's Ferry," Lee reported, "thus opening the line of communication through the Valley. This not having occurred, it became necessary to dislodge the enemy from those positions before concentrating the army west of the mountains."

The verdict on the part of the Union high command to not abandon the two posts did not come without angst. When word first reached Washington of Confederate troops fording the Potomac River, the Union high command realized the possibility that Miles's garrison would be attacked greatly increased. George McClellan wanted the garrisons to leave their positions, or at least move them to the more defensible Maryland Heights overlooking Harpers

▲ Brigadier General Julius White had an interesting career during the Civil War. After the Maryland Campaign, a court of inquiry acquitted him for his actions at Harpers Ferry. He led a division in the Knoxville Campaign, then was sent back east with Burnside and served as his chief of staff through the battle of the Crater. He continued to serve with the Ninth Corps until it was disbanded, then White resigned from the military. (Library of Congress)

◀ Major General Henry Halleck was considered one of the smartest military strategists in the Federal army. After his success in northern Mississippi in the spring of 1862, Lincoln called him east to be the general-in-chief of the United States armies on July 23. Halleck served well in the role of an administrator but was not effective in leading the Union war effort and strategy. (Library of Congress)

Ferry. General-in-Chief Henry Halleck, however, determined not to abandon Harpers Ferry and the United States supplies there. He turned management of the garrisons over to Middle Department commander John Wool. Several times between September 5 and 7, Halleck and Wool stressed the importance to White and Miles of them holding their positions. Wool told White, "defend yourself to the last extremity" while Halleck stated unequivocally to Miles: "You will not abandon Harpers Ferry without defending it to the last extremity." These strict orders put Miles, White, and the troops under their command in the crosshairs of the Army of Northern Virginia and forced Lee to change his campaign plans.

On September 9, with his hands bandaged from an earlier fall that left him unable to write the orders himself, Lee dictated the army's plans for the next few days to one of his staff officers. Special Orders No. 191 gave detailed instructions to Lee's principal subordinates. In ten numbered paragraphs, Lee laid out his strategy.

"Stonewall" Jackson's three divisions would spearhead the army's advance the next morning in the direction of Hagerstown, 25 miles northwest of Frederick. Jackson's men would not advance to the town itself. Instead, he was told to "cross the Potomac at the most convenient point" and, by Friday, September 12, occupy the Baltimore and Ohio Railroad at Martinsburg, capture the enemy there, "and intercept such as may attempt to escape from Harper's Ferry."

James Longstreet and his two divisions received orders to follow Jackson's route as far as Boonsboro and stop there with the army's wagon trains. Daniel H. Hill's division, the army's rear guard, was also to march towards Boonsboro.

Two divisions jointly under Lafayette McLaws—his own and that of Major General

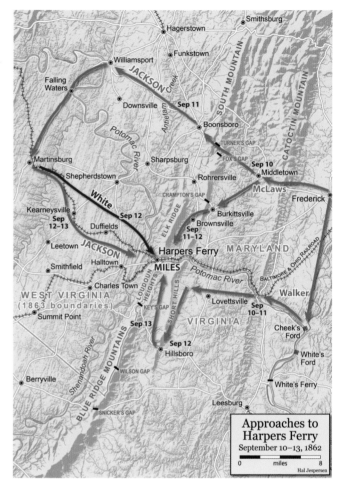

Richard Anderson—were tasked with occupying Maryland Heights by the morning of September 12 and subduing Miles's garrison from the north. Brigadier General John Walker's division received the task of occupying Loudoun Heights at the same time before cooperating with Jackson and McLaws to "intercept [the] retreat of the enemy."

Once Jackson's, McLaws', and Walker's commands completed their goals, they were ordered to "join the main body of the army at Boonsboro or Hagerstown" and put Lee's reunited army in a position to push north into Pennsylvania.

Lee tasked Major General J. E. B. Stuart's cavalry with screening the army's march

▶ Today, the location of the Best Farm is a rural oasis in the rapidly growing city of Frederick, Maryland, as part of the Monocacy National Battlefield Park. Many theories suggest that the Best Farm is the location where Federals discovered Lee's "Lost Orders," while more modern theories place the location closer to Frederick. (Author's collection)

and watching for advancing Federal troops from the direction of Washington.

Special Orders No. 191 called for Lee's infantry to split into four parts. Three of them, about 24,000 men in all, were charged with opening Lee's intended communication and supply line: the Shenandoah Valley.

In plotting his army's next move, General Lee made two assumptions about his strategy. Both dealt with the element of time.

First, Lee trusted his officers and men to wrap up operations in the Shenandoah Valley quickly—just three days. This belief was likely fueled by the confidence Lee had in his soldiers. Also, according to Lafayette McLaws, Lee downplayed a report that "there was a force of 7000 or 8000 men in garrison at Harper's Ferry; but he was inclined to think the number was exaggerated, and that there was not, perhaps, more than 3000 or 4000." Surely, the three divisions of McLaws, Anderson, and Walker—approximately 18,000 men— would be strong enough to speedily dispense with a force of that size.

Lee's second assumption about time was that he had plenty of it before any enemy force would move against him from Washington. He believed the army under McClellan's command was "in a very demoralized and chaotic condition, and will not be prepared for offensive operations—or he will not think it so— for three or four weeks." Throughout the Army of Northern Virginia's top brass, "The hallucination that McClellan was not capable of serious work seemed to pervade our army," said James Longstreet after the war. Nonetheless, Lee set a quick timetable for his men to complete their missions and reunite.

On the morning of September 10, at 4:00 a.m., Jackson's column began marching west from Frederick. The march through the cramped streets of Frederick consumed at least 16 hours that day. Jackson's three divisions crested Catoctin Mountain five miles west of the city before passing through Middletown, whose Union-leaning citizenry unabashedly let the Confederates know of their sympathies.

After surmounting South Mountain at Turner's Gap, the Confederates advanced another five miles further and reaching the outskirts of Boonsboro at the mountain's western base. Jackson paused his men's march with his command straddling the mountain.

The rest of Lee's divisions were slow to squeeze out of the tight confines of Frederick's streets. Longstreet's and D. H. Hill's divisions trailed Jackson and failed to advance over South Mountain. The two divisions under McLaws's command reached Burkittsville at the base of the South Mountain pass called Crampton's Gap while Walker's men managed to make it across the Potomac River to its south bank.

Lee's columns left the mediocre marching exhibited of September 10 in the dust the next day. Jackson, having decided to cross the Potomac at Williamsport instead of near Sharpsburg, pushed the van of his three divisions to a point seven miles west of Martinsburg after trekking his men an average of 23 miles on September 11.

The road opened by Jackson's march allowed Longstreet's men an easy day to reach Boonsboro, their objective. However, Lee deviated from Special Orders No. 191 and ordered Longstreet's divisions to press onto Hagerstown, thus dividing his army into five pieces. There, a supply of flour awaited the Confederates, who would also be in a position to stop enemy troops rumored to be in Chambersburg, Pennsylvania, from disrupting his plans. Longstreet's lead brigade entered Hagerstown that same day while the rest completed the Confederate occupation of the town on September 12.

D. H. Hill's troops, now the sole rear guard for the army, bivouacked on the east side of Turner's Gap. McLaws crossed his columns over South Mountain and debouched into Pleasant Valley between that mountain and

Elk Ridge, which terminated as Maryland Heights overlooking Harpers Ferry. Walker's division remained south of Point of Rocks.

Stuart's cavalry screen was still east of Frederick sparring with Federal cavalry when the army's operations began on September 10. The next day, he constricted his line closer to Frederick. Doing so took him out of contact with the enemy forces opposing him.

Friday, September 12, saw Lee's army disperse further. Longstreet's force occupied Hagerstown while Jackson's divisions pushed Julius White's garrison out of Martinsburg. Those Federals fell back to Harpers Ferry, increasing the garrison's strength there to approximately 14,000. White, who outranked Miles, ceded command to the more experienced

▲ J. E. B. Stuart and his cavalry excelled at providing accurate intelligence to Robert E. Lee. His performance in the Maryland Campaign in this respect was, however, lackluster. (Library of Congress)

▲ The saddle in the mountains is Solomon's Gap. Here, Confederate forces under Barksdale and Kershaw accessed Maryland Heights. Using a cart path, thousands of Confederates slowly climbed the heights and headed south towards Harpers Ferry. (Author's collection)

colonel. In the meantime, Walker's division continued its trudge, moving to within a day's march of Loudoun Heights.

McLaws's command had the toughest day of any of the Confederate forces who were part of the Valley Expedition. McLaws stretched all but two of his brigades across the floor of Pleasant Valley and the spine of South Mountain before advancing them towards the Potomac. This sealed off escape routes to the north for Miles's troops. In the meantime, brigadier generals William Barksdale's and Joseph Kershaw's brigades ascended Elk Ridge via Solomon's Gap, four miles north of Harpers Ferry. They fought the mountain's terrain and advanced to a point about a mile north of Elk Ridge's summit before darkness and stout enemy

▶ The Federal line at Bolivar Heights was a formidable position, especially from the west. Dozens of Federal artillery lined these heights. For all of these defensive efforts, Bolivar was not indefensible from Maryland or Loudoun Heights, where enemy artillery could rain havoc from the east. (Author's collection)

resistance convinced Kershaw to delay the action until the next day.

With Jackson, Walker, and McLaws closing in on him, Dixon Miles finalized his positions for the coming fight. Maryland Heights towered highest over Harpers Ferry. There, Miles placed Colonel Thomas Ford and his 1,150-man brigade in command. Despite orders to the contrary, Miles had not fortified the heights, leaving a tall task for Ford, Ohio's former lieutenant governor and not an experienced military man.

The second-tallest mountain surrounding Harpers Ferry—Loudoun Heights—Miles left unoccupied. He believed it would be impossible for the enemy to place its artillery there and did not want to waste his scant garrison guarding it.

Miles believed that if any enemy column should advance to Harpers Ferry—and he was skeptical that it would—the main attack would come from the west against Bolivar Heights. Intelligence told him this, and thus that is where Miles stretched his main line of defense. These heights were imposing from the valley floor west of them. They stood over 300 feet above the ground immediately to the west and 180 feet over the crest of Schoolhouse Ridge one and a quarter mile in the same direction. However, as on Maryland Heights, Miles neglected ordering the construction of any fortifications on Bolivar Heights.

Bolivar Heights's strength was not just that it was a tall ridgeline. It also stretched two miles from end to end with its northern flank anchored on the Potomac River and its southern tip commanding the Shenandoah River. Miles's limited strength did not allow the two brigades he assigned to his main line of defense—colonels Frederick D'Utassy's and William Trimble's as well as 12 guns in two batteries—to reach from end to end. Instead, believing the ground on the

south end of the heights to be "impassable" because of that sector's broken terrain, Miles condensed D'Utassy's and Trimble's lines to cover 1.3 miles of the two-mile heights, leaving the southern end empty. A third brigade under Colonel William Ward defended Camp Hill one mile to the rear of Bolivar Heights.

Miles's defenses were laid out by the time his advanced forces on Maryland Heights clashed with the lead elements of Kershaw's brigade on September 12. Besides sparring with Ford's pickets, Kershaw's men, followed by Barksdale's Mississippians, had to contend with Elk Ridge's terrain without the aid of cavalry or artillery. "The men had to pull themselves up precipitous inclines by the twigs and undergrowth that lined the mountain side," wrote one of Kershaw's men. Kershaw himself admitted, "The natural obstacles were so great" that his brigade could not even make it to the summit of the mountain by dusk on September 12.

A volley from behind Federal works atop the mountain also stalled the Confederate advance. Ford's men had begun constructing them on September 11. By the time Kershaw's men came face to face with them, the defensive positions erected by the Federals were formidable despite the limited time Ford and his men had to construct them. Two stretches of abatis—"trees cut down and limbs sharpened at the ends and all piled up in a mass"—were amassed north of a breastwork made of "large chestnut logs" and other trees "with rocks to shoot through," providing Ford's men with cover from enemy fire. The abatis would slow any enemy assault while the mountain's steep slopes secured the Union flanks.

Ford's position on the mountain was not impervious, however. He dispersed his command to many points along the Maryland shore and mountain and

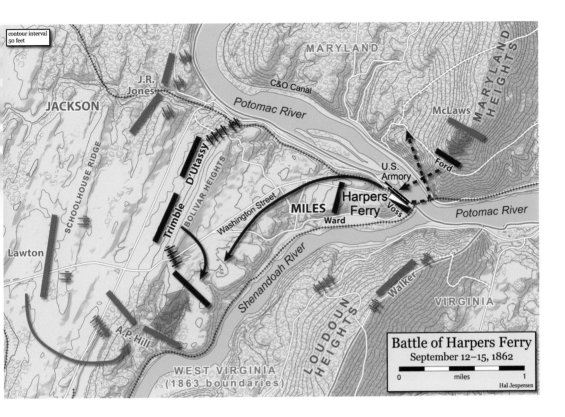

cannibalized the regiments under his command, diminishing unit cohesion.

Below the mountain in Pleasant Valley, McLaws's columns sealed off Miles's escape routes to the north. On Elk Ridge, Kershaw's men spent a fitful night on the mountain within earshot of the 640 Federal defenders behind their breastwork.

When the sun rose on September 13, volleys of musketry erupted between the two weary sides. Ford's men at the breastwork loaded and fired with a determination that again stalled Kershaw's advance. At a distance of 100 yards, the opposing lines blazed away at one another. Kershaw called on Barksdale for assistance. The Mississippians struggled fighting the contours, briars, and rocks of the mountain. Incredibly, they were able to get in position on the Federal right.

As Barksdale's men moved into place, the commander of the green 126th New York, Colonel Eliakim Sherrill, took a Confederate bullet to the jaw, badly mangling his face and mouth. In their first fight, this unhinged the New Yorkers who, hastened by a precipitate volley from some of Barksdale's men, fled their position at the breastwork, carrying the rest of the Union line with them. By 10:30 a.m., four hours after the fighting commenced, McLaws's mountain men secured the enemy works.

Down the mountain slope, aides and officers feverishly worked to rally the broken companies. Some of the soldiers driven back from the breastwork rallied a quarter mile south of their old position. Dixon Miles himself rode to Maryland Heights to make sense of the situation and speak with Ford. There, Ford expressed the belief that he could not hold onto Maryland Heights. "You can and you must," Miles shot back. The mountain—the key to Harpers Ferry—was still in Federal possession.

31

Believing the situation calmed, Miles returned to Bolivar Heights, but not before giving Ford discretionary orders that if his troops "gave way once again," he could withdraw them from Maryland Heights. For the next three hours, neither side seriously tested the other's position. Bullets still sliced through the wooded mountain, but no coordinated attacks came.

From his headquarters below the summit, Ford clamored for more reinforcements while trying to make sense of what was happening at the front. Reports told him of confusion and disorder among the Federal regiments on Maryland Heights. Then word reached him that no more reinforcements could be spared as Jackson's Confederates had begun arriving west of Bolivar Heights. Armed with discretion, Ford ordered a withdrawal. "You are hereby ordered to fall back to Harper's Ferry in good order," the brief order stated. "Be careful to do so in good order."

At 3:30 p.m., from his command post across the Potomac River, Miles's attention was drawn to Maryland Heights. He saw a stream of blue-coated soldiers moving down the mountain. "God Almighty!" he blurted out. "What does that mean? They are coming down. Hell and damnation!"

The men of Miles's garrison shared their commanders dread and shock. Regarding Ford's order, one 126th New York soldier said, "Had an order been given to surrender to the enemy, we should not have been more surprised; for in abandoning that position, we saw plainly that everything was lost." One of General White's aides wrote that after the loss of Maryland Heights, "the game was clearly up with us." Miles, however disheartened he was about the loss of the heights, did not wave the white flag yet. He assumed the enemy could do little damage with their artillery from Maryland and Loudoun Heights. He buttressed his

main line of defense on Bolivar Heights and prepared to hold out. Time was running out for Miles and his men.

While Ford was left to determine the fate of Maryland Heights, Miles had other Confederate forces closing in on Harpers Ferry to contend with. Despite his assumptions about the impossibility of enemy troops mounting Loudoun Heights, elements of Brig. Gen. John Walker's division had done so on September 13. To make matters worse, by noon that same day, Jackson's three divisions reached Schoolhouse Ridge west of Bolivar Heights. Miles and his men were hemmed in from the west, north, and south, effectively eliminating any chance of escape. Miles, however, did not favor escaping. His orders were to hold Harpers Ferry, and that is what he would do.

He was not blind to his worsening situation, however, and he dispatched a rider to "try to reach somebody that had ever heard of the United States Army, or any general of the United States Army, or anybody that knew anything about the United States Army, and report the condition of Harper's Ferry." Miles hoped his rider would find someone more specific than his instructions let on: Maj. Gen. George B. McClellan. If found, Miles's courier was to inform McClellan that the Harpers Ferry garrison could only hold out for 48 more hours.

McClellan was on his way. By September 13, he was within a two days' march of Harpers Ferry, if unopposed. But the divided Army of Northern Virginia stood between the two Union forces. Since September 9, McClellan had been moving his army towards Frederick while trying to divine the enemy's location and intentions and accomplish his objective of protecting Washington and Baltimore. On September 11, the Army of the Potomac occupied

▶ Though only 800 feet high, Sugarloaf Mountain is more noticeable because it is not part of a nearby mountain chain. It is referred to as a monadnock, an isolated mountain rising abruptly from level surrounding land. The mountain played a significant role in the Civil War as a lookout/signal station in several campaigns. (Author's collection)

two important terrain features needed to achieve those aims.

That Thursday, soldiers of the Ninth Corps seized Parr's Ridge, an 830-foot eminence that was the tallest piece of ground along the National Road between Baltimore and Frederick, without a fight. Fourteen miles southwest, Union troops had to pry Sugarloaf Mountain away from the Confederates defending it.

As early as September 9, McClellan ordered his cavalry chief Pleasonton to occupy the mountain. Pleasonton sent a small cavalry force accompanied by two pieces of artillery to drive Colonel Thomas Munford's two cavalry regiments and artillery battery away from the mountain's base. The first attempt failed on September 10.

McClellan ordered Franklin's corps and Major General Darius Couch's division—attached to the Sixth Corps—to lend immediate support and drive the Confederate cavalry away from Sugarloaf Mountain. No further attempts were made on September 10, but McClellan reiterated his orders to Franklin for the next day, telling him "the earlier we gain the Sugar

Loaf the better." By the afternoon of September 11, with Lee's columns moving west from Frederick and Stuart's cavalry screen consolidating closer to that city, Munford had only a rear guard at the base of Sugarloaf. Colonel John Farnsworth's cavalry brigade, backed up by a brigade of Sixth Corps infantry, dislodged the remainder of Munford's troopers and secured the prominent overlook.

Shortly after the Army of the Potomac's seizure of Parr's Ridge and Sugarloaf Mountain, information reached McClellan's headquarters of the Confederate abandonment of Frederick. Additionally, this intelligence, provided by Pennsylvania governor Andrew Curtin, stated that Confederate troops were in Hagerstown just south of the Maryland–Pennsylvania line. Having accomplished his first campaign objective of protecting Washington and Baltimore, McClellan ordered a movement to Frederick the next day "to follow him [the enemy] into Pennsylvania if necessary." "It was now determined to move more rapidly," said Ninth Corps division commander Jacob

Cox, whose Ohioans would spearhead the movement on Frederick on September 12.

Now sure of the enemy in his front, McClellan asked for additional troops to aid him in the coming struggle. Besides requesting reinforcements from Washington, McClellan also inquired of Henry Halleck if Miles's garrison at Harpers Ferry could join the Army of the Potomac. Halleck, intent on holding the town and the supplies there, said Miles could not join McClellan's army until "you can open communications with him. When you do so, he will be subject to your orders." Thus, McClellan dispatched orders for his army to move on September 12.

Ambrose Burnside's right wing was in the best position to occupy Frederick that day. The men of the Ninth Corps in the lead tried to shield themselves from the morning rain as they marched. One soldier said marching in such conditions was "painfully laborious," but they continued on. The people of New Market, a town along the National Road less than eight miles east of Frederick, turned out to greet the Federal soldiers, lessening the labors of the march for a bit. In particular, four young ladies greeted the Union troops by waving a newly made flag. "New Market is a fine little town," one infantryman concluded.

A little over halfway between New Market and Frederick, the Jug Bridge carried the National Road over the Monocacy River. After noon, Cox's men approached the bridge, when they came under fire. Brigadier General Wade Hampton's brigade remained in Frederick as Lee's army marched west. He positioned his cavalry and three artillery pieces to oppose any Federals trying to cross the Monocacy River.

Cox responded to the artillery fire by ordering up his own artillery to add their metal to the fight. As the two sides banged away at each other, Cox deployed his infantry to break the impasse. Colonel Augustus Moor's Ohioans headed straight

▲ The Jug Bridge derived its name from the stone "demijohn" that sat on the east side of the bridge. It was constructed in 1808. The bridge abutments still stand on either side of the Monocacy River. (Library of Congress)

for the bridge while another Ohio regiment forded the river to the north. The pressure convinced Hampton he could no longer hold the river crossing. He gave orders for his troopers to withdraw into Frederick.

By 5:00 p.m., Moor's brigade, with its commander in the lead, pursued Hampton's horsemen. At a bend in the road in the eastern end of Frederick, Hampton's men turned around and attacked Moor's troops. A swirling melee in the city's tight streets broke out. The Federals even brought a cannon into the fight, which fired into the closely packed streets now full of mounted soldiers. Hampton's men got the best of the fight, putting some hesitation in the enemy advance. In the confusing fight, Moor became a prisoner of Hampton's brigade. Having bought enough time for the rest of his brigade to leave the city, Hampton withdrew to Middletown and Catoctin Mountain west of Frederick, leaving the town in Federal hands. Cox's men entered it to the jubilation of many of its Unionist citizens.

The rest of the Army of the Potomac made commendable gains marching on September 12. By the end of the day, most units were within an easy march of Frederick's spired skyline. During the army's advance to Frederick, George McClellan received numerous reports about Confederate activity in Maryland. On the morning of September 12, he reported to Henry Halleck, "My columns are pushing on rapidly to Frederick. I feel perfectly confident that the enemy has abandoned Frederick moving in two directions. Viz. on the Hagerstown & Harpers Ferry roads." By nightfall, besides receiving information that

the van of Burnside's wing entered Frederick, McClellan still could not sort out the intentions of the enemy. What did it mean that they moved in two different directions: to the north towards Williamsport and to the south towards Harpers Ferry? "My movements tomorrow will be dependent upon information to be received during the night," he informed Halleck.

McClellan also attempted to open communication with the Harpers Ferry garrison so that they would, as Halleck had agreed, be under his command. He told Halleck that though he had not heard the distant boom of cannon in that direction, "in my orders of movement for tomorrow [September 13] have arranged so that I go or send to his relief if necessary."

As for Lee, the Confederate commander accompanied two divisions of James Longstreet's command to Hagerstown (this movement was not part of Special Orders No. 191, as noted above). There, Lee did not receive the news he expected to on September 12. No couriers galloped to him with news of Harpers Ferry's fall. Instead, his cavalryman J. E. B. Stuart reported via D. H. Hill at Boonsboro that the enemy was advancing on Frederick. This was unsettling news for Lee, who had assumed the Union army was days—maybe weeks—away from such a movement. While in Hagerstown, he would have to wait for more news— any news—about the progress of Jackson's columns in suppressing Harpers Ferry. Until then, all he could do was monitor the enemy movements. The campaign that Lee had begun with much hope and promise was beginning to slip from his bandaged hands.

# September 13, A Day of Decision

September 13, 1862, was a critical day in the Maryland Campaign. Lee's army, still divided, was spread over 20 miles of Maryland and Virginia countryside. McClellan's forces closed within a day's march of the Army of Northern Virginia and prepared to meet it and drive it from Maryland.

Reveille for the Army of the Potomac stirred its members awake before dawn on September 13. The soldiers wiped the sleep from their eyes, buttoned their coats, slung on their accoutrements, shouldered their weapons, and formed into column on the roads leading to Frederick.

In the van of the Twelfth Corps were the men of the 27th Indiana Infantry. Orders to march rang out along the column, and the formations stepped forward. What this day would bring was unknown to the men of the regiment. All they knew was that the enemy army was somewhere in front of them in the area of Frederick. "We were liable at any time to encounter rebel scouts or outposts," one Indianan remembered. At least for the men from the Hoosier State, they were on familiar roads and ground. They had spent the previous winter camped in the area. Yet the prospect of battle hung over the Indianans. Marching along familiar roads and passing recognizable landmarks provided the men with a sense of security and stirred memories of their time in camp. Now, they were on campaign, "where the sudden and violent changes

which the fortunes of war may bring about were forcibly impressed upon us."

The Indianans fell out of ranks in a field on the outskirts of Frederick. Sergeant John Bloss and Corporal Barton W. Mitchell of the regiment found a wheatfield and laid down in it. Soon after stretching themselves out on the trodden wheat, Mitchell saw an envelope sitting beneath a tree. Curious, he stood up, walked to the tree, and stooped down to grab the item left behind by the Confederate army. In the envelope, Mitchell saw a letter folded around two cigars. He glanced at the letter and then handed it to Sgt. Bloss, who, after reading it in full, quickly passed the document—a lost partial copy of Lee's Special Orders No. 191—up the chain of command.

The Lost Orders—as they've come to be known—passed through Twelfth Corps headquarters. There, staffer Samuel Pittman said he recognized the signature at the bottom of it, that of Lee's chief of staff Robert Chilton. Pittman became familiar with Chilton's signature from his days working in a Detroit bank, where Chilton, an army paymaster at a nearby post, deposited checks. Confirmed as genuine,

## Who Lost the Lost Orders?

This is a question that has been asked—and never satisfactorily answered with certainty—since the conclusion of the Maryland Campaign. The copy that fell into Federal hands was addressed from army headquarters to Maj. Gen. D. H. Hill. Hill was adequately defended by his staff during the postwar finger-pointing by swearing under oath that the only copy of Special Orders No. 191 that he received was from "Stonewall" Jackson's headquarters. Procedures for tracking orders of this nature and ensuring they arrived where they were supposed to were in place at army headquarters, but it seems that they were lacking in being properly carried out. Who the blame of losing the orders should ultimately rest with may never be known.

The "Lost Orders" can now be found in George B. McClellan's papers at the Library of Congress. Its discovery is probably one of the best-known, and least understood, stories of the Civil War. (Library of Congress)

▲ The reactions of Frederick's citizens to the Army of the Potomac's arrival in their town proved to be a more widespread and joyous occasion than when the Army of Northern Virginia arrived days earlier. (Library of Congress)

the orders continued up the ladder to George McClellan himself.

Frederick's tightly packed streets funneled the Army of the Potomac into the town as it approached from the east and southeast. Traffic jams slowed the army as it marched through the city. Joyous citizens, many expressing their happiness over being free from Confederate occupation, came into the streets in droves to welcome the Army of the Potomac and its commanding general. "I was nearly overwhelmed & pulled to pieces," McClellan admitted to his wife. After reviewing his troops and passing through the serenading mass of citizens, McClellan traveled to the west end of the city. Between 2:00 and 3:00 p.m., the Lost Orders came into his hands.

While Mitchell's discovery has often been hailed as a magnificently lucky and fortunate discovery for McClellan, the Lost Orders were not perfect. Firstly, the copy, made out to D. H. Hill, was four days old and called for the disparate portions of Lee's army to complete their objectives by Friday, September 12. It was Saturday, September 13, when McClellan read them. Second, each paragraph in the orders was numbered, and the first paragraph on this copy was labeled number three. Two paragraphs were missing. Lastly, Hagerstown was only mentioned twice in the order: once as a road and once as the possible point of reunification for the Army of Northern Virginia. But McClellan had positive information that the enemy—at least some of it—was in Hagerstown. Was the order deviated from? Or had that meant the army had reunited already?

The Lost Orders did explain to the Union general why his intelligence was reporting the enemy moving in two different directions. He believed, not wrongly, that the questions stemming from the document outweighed the answers. Seeking more answers, at 3:00 p.m., McClellan passed the order to his cavalry chief Alfred Pleasonton. McClellan "desires you to

## Profile: Major General George B. McClellan, 1826–85

George Brinton McClellan was born to a prominent Philadelphia, Pennsylvania, family on December 3, 1826. He attended schools in Pennsylvania at a young age before being appointed to West Point. McClellan graduated second in the Class of 1846 and received an assignment to the army's Corps of Engineers. In the Mexican War, McClellan served on General Winfield Scott's staff and received two brevet promotions. Following the war, he taught at the United States Military Academy at West Point and continued in various engineering duties. Following a stint as a member of a board of officers to observe the Crimean War, McClellan resigned his United States Army commission. He served as the chief engineer of two Midwestern railroad companies. Appointed to command of all Ohio volunteers at the Civil War's outset, McClellan's victories in western Virginia quickly vaulted him to command of the Army of the Potomac and all United States

armies. McClellan spent the winter of 1861–62 dictating Union war policy and morphing the Army of the Potomac into an efficient fighting force. The general took his army to the Virginia Peninsula in the spring of 1862 and advanced on Richmond. Part of his army remained behind to defend Washington under the orders of President Abraham Lincoln and Secretary of War Edwin Stanton. This caused a rift in the relationship between McClellan and his superiors. Nonetheless, by the end of June 1862, McClellan had moved his army within seven miles of Richmond. Confederates drove McClellan's army away from Richmond during the Seven Days Campaign. McClellan asked for reinforcements to renew his advance on the Confederate capital. Instead, newly appointed General-in-Chief Henry Halleck ordered McClellan to bring his army back to Northern Virginia to unite with Maj. Gen. John Pope's Army of Virginia. Following Pope's defeat at the battle of Second Manassas, President Lincoln appointed McClellan to command the Army of the Potomac to defeat the Confederate invasion of Maryland. McClellan achieved two victories in Maryland in September 1862 at South Mountain and Antietam. Against Lincoln's wishes, he took six weeks to prepare his army for the next campaign in Virginia. McClellan did not satisfy Lincoln's expectations in the Loudoun Valley Campaign and was removed from command. He became the Democrats' candidate for the presidency in the Election of 1864 but lost to Lincoln. After the war, he served one term as New Jersey's governor. McClellan died on October 29, 1885.

► George B. McClellan. (Library of Congress)

ascertain whether this order of march has thus far been followed by the enemy," the query stated. It took between 90 and 120 minutes for the bearer of McClellan's note to find Pleasonton, who was currently driving Stuart's cavalry back towards South Mountain. Thirty-five minutes later, even before Pleasonton could verify the contents of the Lost Order, McClellan ordered the army's lead elements west to Middletown, five miles east of South Mountain's crest.

Earlier in the day, while McClellan and his army passed through the throngs of Frederick's Union-loving citizens, Pleasonton had his hands full trying to pierce J. E. B. Stuart's cavalry screen. Pleasonton's horsemen trotted west from their bivouacs around Frederick by dawn. About two miles outside the city, salvos from two Confederate guns fired upon them.

Confederate Lieutenant Colonel William Martin, his Jeff Davis Legion, and two guns guarded Hagan's Gap, the notch in Catoctin Mountain through which the National Road passed. The warm greeting from Martin's guns forced Pleasonton's troopers off the road. Two artillery batteries came forward to contend with Martin's men. More of Hampton's brigade reinforced the mountain pass position. For the better part of the morning and early afternoon, Pleasonton's westward movement was stalled at the base of Catoctin Mountain. Slowly though, his cavalrymen, now dismounted, worked their way up the mountain. By 2:00 p.m., they succeeded in finally driving Martin's force from the gap.

The Confederates reeled down the western slope of the mountain, turning around several times to keep the Federals at bay. Pleasonton's troopers continued driving Stuart's screen back through Middletown and beyond Catoctin Creek on the town's west end. Stuart ended the day at the base

of Turner's Gap in South Mountain, where he found Colquitt's brigade of D. H. Hill's division taking position. Alfred Pleasonton pursued that far, but the impregnability of the position stopped any further efforts to drive the enemy cavalry.

Further south, portions of Pleasonton's command also drove Confederate cavalry through Jefferson Pass in Catoctin Mountain. They pursued the gray-clad horse soldiers to Burkittsville at the east base of Crampton's Gap in South Mountain.

Pleasonton's success and subsequent reconnaissance of the enemy's positions convinced him and McClellan, too, that the lost copy of Special Orders No. 191 was genuine and that Lee's army was

▼ William Franklin graduated first in West Point's Class of 1843. At the beginning of the Civil War, Franklin supervised the construction of the Capitol dome in Washington, DC. (Library of Congress)

still divided. Echoes of gunfire from the direction of Harpers Ferry further confirmed this.

At 6:20 p.m., the army commander laid out his plans for the next day. The verbiage of the Lost Orders placed Lee's main body at Boonsboro at the west base of Turner's Gap (McClellan did not know that Longstreet's two divisions marched to Hagerstown, reducing this force solely to D. H. Hill's five brigades). Thus, McClellan put the weight of his army on the National Road for the next day's march. Burnside's wing—the First and Ninth corps—spearheaded the move to that gap. Supporting columns consisting of Sumner's Second Corps, Williams's Twelfth Corps, and Sykes' Fifth Corps division

▼ Alfred Colquitt graduated from Princeton University in 1844. He served as a postwar governor of Georgia and a United States senator. (Library of Congress)

followed. With this heavy force, McClellan intended to hold the enemy's main body in position. To the south, much of his plan's success or failure rested on the shoulders of Sixth Corps commander Maj. Gen. William B. Franklin.

McClellan asked of Franklin "at this important moment all your intellect & the utmost activity that a general can exercise." Armed with those traits, McClellan hoped Franklin could complete the main purpose of the plan: "to cut the enemy in two & beat him in detail." The best way to do that, McClellan felt, was to hold the enemy's main force at Boonsboro, allowing Franklin's corps to serve as the hammer delivering blows to the divided Army of Northern Virginia. Franklin received orders to push through South Mountain and move into Pleasant Valley to trap McLaws's two divisions between Franklin's force and the still-fighting Union garrison at Harpers Ferry. Geography played against McLaws here too, as South Mountain to his east and Elk Ridge to his west would hem him in a four-sided box with no means of escape. Once Franklin destroyed McLaws's two divisions and relieved Miles's force, he was either to move north to Boonsboro and aid in the fight there or turn west and cut off the enemy's retreat across the Potomac River. It was a lot to ask of Franklin, but McClellan had faith in the plan. Portions of the Ninth Corps marched into position a few miles from Turner's Gap after dark. The remainder of the Army of the Potomac slept around Frederick with orders to rise early and be ready for another day's march.

Back at Turner's Gap, J. E. B. Stuart left D. H. Hill with the impression that Colquitt's brigade was sufficient to handle the enemy directly in his front. He passed along a similar report to Lee at Hagerstown before heading south believing that the main Federal effort to relieve Harpers Ferry

41

would come through one of the passes closer to the Potomac River. With his army still divided, Lee was worried about the enemy's movements west of Frederick. Then, that night, another report arrived from D. H. Hill that further darkened his outlook.

When the sun set behind the western slope of the mountain, darkening the Middletown Valley, Colquitt's men looked at the valley floor below them. Thousands of campfires flickered. There was a much stronger force in front of them than Stuart said, it seemed. Colquitt informed Hill and asked for help, which came in the form of Brig. Gen. Samuel Garland's North Carolina brigade and Capt. John Lane's battery. Hill then passed along Colquitt's report to Lee.

Lee admitted a few days later "that the enemy was advancing more rapidly than convenient" for him and his plans. He had to adjust them quickly to avert disaster. If the Federals brushed aside Hill's lone division at Turner's Gap, they could turn south and trap McLaws in Pleasant Valley—two whole divisions of the Army of Northern Virginia. That was a loss Lee could not risk. To prevent it, he ordered Longstreet's two divisions at Hagerstown to retrace their steps towards Boonsboro and support Hill from a position behind Beaver Creek about three miles northwest of the town.

Longstreet's men did not begin their march until the next morning. Tens of thousands of Union and Confederate soldiers were poised the next day to fight the first major clash north of the Potomac River on the rugged slopes of South Mountain.

# Fire on the Mountains

At Harpers Ferry and three mountain gaps in South Mountain, artillery and musketry fire and the smoke they created engulfed the landscape. Lee's army fought for time, McClellan's to drive Lee from Maryland and relieve Harpers Ferry.

Daniel Harvey Hill reached Turner's Gap "between daylight and sunrise" on the cool morning of Sunday, September 14, 1862. Atop the mountain beside the National Road stood the stone Mountain Inn. Near the building, Hill found Samuel Garland's North Carolinians waiting for orders and delayed issuing any until he had more information of the ground. The division commander rode to Colquitt's line east of Turner's Gap and adjusted it by withdrawing it further up the mountain slope and then ordered the rest of his division to the gap. In the growing daylight, he then departed Turner's Gap and rode south.

Hill and one of his staff officers used the Wood Road to survey his right flank. One mile south of Turner's Gap, the Old Sharpsburg Road crossed the mountain at Fox's Gap. When he arrived just north of there, Hill heard "the voices of commands and the rumbling of wheels," an ominous sign that Federals already held this important gap on Hill's right. Hill returned north to find troops to send to retake Fox's Gap.

On his way north, he interviewed a mountain dweller to get a feel for the terrain and road network of the Turner's Gap area. Hill learned the enormity of his task. To defend Turner's Gap, he not only had to defend that mountain pass but three others, too: Fox's Gap that he had just approached one mile south, Frostown Gap one mile north of Turner's, and Orr's Gap two miles further north of Frostown. This information and his reconnaissances of the position convinced Hill that the Turner's Gap sector "could only be held by a large force, and was wholly indefensible by a small one." Hill's 8,000 men had five miles of mountain slope to cover.

▶ Daniel Harvey Hill performed well commanding his division at South Mountain and Antietam, but his prickly personality extended to his comrades as well as to his enemies. (John Hugh Reynolds Photographs, ca. 1879–1910, MS R33, Box 1, Image 64. Special Collections, University of Arkansas Libraries, Fayetteville)

Upon his return to the Mountain House, Hill dispatched Garland's five North Carolina regiments—1,100 strong—to Fox's Gap. Once Garland's men reclaimed it from the enemy, Hill told him to "hold it at all hazards," an assignment no commander wanted to hear. Garland saluted and turned his column south, moving quietly and anxiously along the Wood Road with the expectation of Union troops in their front.

But Garland found gray-clad troopers—not Union infantry—occupied Fox's Gap. Stuart placed them there before he personally headed south and failed to notify Hill of this arrangement. Garland's brief sigh of relief vanished quickly as he laid out his regiments to defend the gap.

Garland's regiments filed into line. Stuart's cavalrymen and horse artillery section held the extreme right of Garland's line and covered the Loop Road south of the gap. Three North Carolina regiments stretched north towards Fox's Gap and received the support of Bondurant's

battery in the center of Garland's line. The artillerymen partially covered a hole between Garland's center regiment and his two left regiments that he left near the Old Sharpsburg Road. The terrain and road network forced an imperfect disposition upon Garland's brigade that was too small to hold the entirety of the battlefield of Fox's Gap. His 1,100 men occupied 1,300 yards of space. Garland formed his line minutes before 9:00 a.m. They did not have long to wait to see action.

As Hill learned South Mountain's layout, Alfred Pleasonton acquainted himself with the same terrain. His artillery sought out Confederate positions near Turner's Gap. By the time Pleasonton's support arrived in the form of Colonel Eliakim Scammon's 1,500-man brigade, he realized a direct movement against Turner's Gap would not be easy. Accordingly, Pleasonton sent Scammon in the direction of Fox's Gap while division commander Jacob Cox forwarded the rest of the Kanawha

▼ Today's Reno Monument Road follows the path of the wartime Old Sharpsburg Road, which continues straight in this image. Scammon's soldiers, the first Federals to attack Fox's Gap, followed the Loop Road to enter the gap, which is a driveway today but can be seen running towards the left of the photo. The oak tree under which Jesse Reno died stood near the intersection of Reno Monument and Fox Gap roads until the late 20th century. (Author's collection)

▲ Samuel Garland graduated from both the Virginia Military Institute and the University of Virginia prior to the outbreak of war. Division commander D. H. Hill lamented that Garland "had no superiors and few equals in the service." (Library of Congress)

his column off the Old Sharpsburg Road onto the Loop Road to envelop the right of the enemy's line that held Fox's Gap. His three regiments were in their battle lines shortly before 9:00 a.m.

A few minutes later, Ohioans and North Carolinians opened fire on each other three-quarters of a mile south of Fox's Gap. Garland's rightmost regiment, the 5th North Carolina, advanced to meet Lieutenant Colonel Rutherford B. Hayes's 23rd Ohio on Scammon's left. The two regiments traded sharp volleys before Hayes ordered a charge, which broke the impasse. Garland moved his regiments to the south to buttress his crumbling right flank. They halted Hayes's advance. In the firefight, the future 19th President of the United States went down with a serious wound.

The pressure on Garland's brigade increased as Scammon brought more of his men into the fight against Garland's center and left. Yet the North Carolinians still clung tenaciously to their mountaintop.

Near the left of his line, the mounted Garland approached Colonel Thomas Ruffin and the 13th North Carolina. "General, why do you stay here?" Ruffin asked. "You are in great danger." "I may as well be here as yourself," answered Garland. "No, no, it is my duty to be here with my

Division. Pleasonton envisioned a sweep up the mountain and an assault upon Hill's right at Turner's Gap once these Federals occupied Fox's Gap.

At the foot of Fox's Gap, Scammon's regiments dodged artillery shells raining upon them from the pass. Scammon turned

## Maryland Campaign Presidents

The 23rd Ohio Infantry is sometimes called the "Regiment of Presidents." Two future United States Presidents served in its ranks during the Maryland Campaign and throughout the war: 19th President Rutherford B. Hayes and 25th President William McKinley. Hayes led the regiment at South Mountain, where he was wounded and thus missed the battle of Antietam three days later. Nineteen-year-old William McKinley was the regiment's commissary sergeant. At Antietam, he led wagons of warm food and coffee across the Lower Bridge to feed his comrades. Both men rose through the ranks and continued to serve until the end of the war.

regiment," Ruffin explained, "but you could better superintend your brigade from a safer position." Those words barely left Ruffin's mouth when an enemy bullet hit him in the hip. Moments later, Garland fell too, struck in the chest. He soon died. Ruffin survived.

Once Colonel Duncan McRae learned that he had been elevated to brigade command, the first thing he did was send a courier racing north to D. H. Hill requesting assistance. Hill sent two additional North Carolina units of Brigadier General George B. Anderson's brigade under the command of Colonel Charles Tew. The arrival of reinforcements took some time, however. Meanwhile, McRae's cracking line had to hold.

Eliakim Scammon was becoming frustrated that his men had not secured Fox's Gap as the clock ticked close to 11:00 a.m. If his men could not bust through the enemy line, they would blast through it. At Scammon's request, Cox ordered two Parrott rifles to the front. The guns unlimbered within range of the Tarheel soldiers and only fired four rounds before enough gunners fell for the living to abandon the attempt.

Next, Colonel George Crook's brigade arrived to buttress Scammon's offensive power. The enlarged Federal presence in McRae's and Tew's front stretched the Confederate line and gaps appeared between the regiments. At 11:30 a.m., four regiments from Scammon's and Crook's brigades charged forward with bayonets fixed, yells surging from their throats. Some Confederate units resisted, and it took close quarters, hand to hand fighting to drive them from the field. Once unhinged from their positions, McRae's soldiers fled from Fox's Gap.

The 13th North Carolina found itself surrounded near the Wise cabin in the

confused battle. The wounded Ruffin still led his men. He charged his command against one Ohio regiment first, then turned to face a second before escaping north. They met D. H. Hill and more reinforcements on the way from Turner's Gap, but it was too late. By noon, Cox's Kanawha Division held Fox's Gap.

Following three hours of fighting, Cox was content to hold onto what his men had dearly won. The division lost 324 men. Prisoners warned Cox of Confederate troops to the north. The Ohioans also needed a rest after marching from Middletown just to get to the battlefield and then fighting through the dense woods up South Mountain for three hours.

Even though Cox did not push his division to Turner's Gap, they had

▲ Jacob Cox did not have military experience prior to the start of the Civil War. By September 14, 1862, he commanded a division in the Ninth Corps, and he would tactically command the corps at Antietam three days later. (Library of Congress)

# Profile: Major General James Longstreet, 1821–1904

▲ James Longstreet.
(Library of Congress)

Robert E. Lee's second-in-command during the Maryland Campaign, and much of the war, was born in South Carolina on January 8, 1821. He received his primary education from West Point as a member of the Class of 1842. Like many other West Pointers, Longstreet served in Mexico. He spent the remainder of his pre-Civil War army career in several western posts, resigning from the army at the beginning of the Civil War as a paymaster. Longstreet commanded an infantry brigade during the First Manassas Campaign. His men fought at Blackburn's Ford three days prior to the battle of First Manassas. Personally, Longstreet suffered a tragedy in January 1862 when scarlet fever claimed the lives of three of his four children. The following spring during the Peninsula Campaign, Longstreet fought well at the battle of Williamsburg but did not do the same at the battle of Seven Pines. Longstreet impressed new army commander Lee during the Seven Days Campaign and received command of five of the army's eight divisions during the army's post-campaign reorganization. Lee thought highly of Longstreet's abilities as a commander. Longstreet continued to demonstrate a capacity for sound battlefield decisions at the battle of Second Manassas. There, on August 30, 1862, his wing of the army launched a crushing assault against the enemy's left flank that secured Second Manassas as a resounding Confederate victory. Longstreet's able defensive performances at South Mountain, Antietam, and Fredericksburg complimented his offensive abilities. Longstreet missed the Army of Northern Virginia's next campaign at Chancellorsville. He was in command of Confederate forces around Suffolk, Virginia. Lee's "Old War Horse" was back with the army in time for Gettysburg. There, Longstreet coordinated and led the major Confederate attacks on July 2 and 3. Neither attack was successful. That fall, Longstreet led portions of Lee's army west to support the Army of Tennessee. They participated in the Confederate victory at Chickamauga. Longstreet failed to capture Knoxville, Tennessee, afterward. He returned east in time for the Overland Campaign, but Longstreet did not see much of it. He was wounded by friendly fire during the battle of the Wilderness. When Longstreet recovered and returned to the Army of Northern Virginia, he remained alongside Lee until the surrender of the army at Appomattox Courthouse on April 9, 1865. After the war, Longstreet became a Republican and worked for the United States government, alienating him from many Southerners. He commented extensively about the war until he died on January 2, 1904.

performed good service. Their attacks wrecked Garland's brigade, which lost 212 men killed or wounded and an additional 200 men captured. These casualties were 40 percent of the brigade's strength.

With both commands out of fighting power, the roar of musketry trickled to occasional firing around midday.

While Cox and Hill battled at Fox's Gap, orders from both army commanders of the previous day and the sounds of fighting drew more soldiers to South Mountain. Despite urgings from Longstreet to withdraw Hill from the mountain passes, Lee ordered two divisions under Longstreet's command to march from Hagerstown to Boonsboro to support Hill directly. Longstreet's soldiers left Hagerstown at 8:00 a.m. on September 14. As they marched, heat—the day's high temperature was 73°F—plagued the column as the miles added up. "The day was hot," Longstreet wrote, "and the roads dry and beaten into impalpable powder, that rose in clouds of dust from under our feet as we marched." Choking dust and the warming sun ensured some of Longstreet's men never reached South Mountain; many fell out before getting there.

Longstreet's lead brigade reached Boonsboro at noon. Confused orders, some straight from Lee, forced some of the units to march and countermarch to reach their deployment area. Lee split David R. Jones' division. Brigadier General Thomas Drayton's and Colonel George T. Anderson's brigades went south to Fox's Gap while Jones's remaining three present brigades—Jenkins's, Pickett's, and Kemper's—were slated to fight at Turner's Gap after marching and countermarching 18–20 miles.

John Bell Hood's division was also split. Evans's brigade, led by Colonel Peter Stevens, reinforced Hill's men north of Turner's Gap. Hood's remaining two

brigades was also ordered north of Turner's Gap before being turned around and sent to Fox's Gap.

On the east side of South Mountain, long blue columns tramped their way to the battlefield, too. The remainder of Reno's Ninth Corps led the main body of the Army of the Potomac on the National Road. Brigadier General Orlando Willcox's division was next in the column. Through a miscommunication, Willcox ended up north of the National Road facing Turner's Gap. Right wing commander Ambrose Burnside, who supervised the Federal fights at Turner's and Fox's gaps, corrected Willcox and sent him to the southern gap. Finally, after 2:00 p.m., Willcox's men began deploying next to the Kanawha Division. Brigadier General Samuel Strugis's division reached the front about 3:30 p.m. and Rodman's trailing division joined the rest of the corps an hour later.

As the Ninth Corps prepared to sweep into Turner's Gap from the south, Burnside prepared for a simultaneous assault against the northern approaches to Turner's Gap. The wing commander assigned this task to Maj. Gen. Joseph Hooker's First Corps. Hooker's men rose early that Sunday—3:00 a.m.—and began leaving their camps east of Frederick about daybreak. Following a march of about 15 miles, Hooker's columns deployed into battle lines north of the National Road facing South Mountain. There, the First Corps soldiers got a glimpse of the task ahead of them. South Mountain's slopes, Hooker said, "are precipitous, rugged, and wooded, and difficult of ascent to an infantry force, even in absence of a foe in front." The First Corps soldiers had little time to ponder the tough task in front of them before the Union assaults renewed against Turner's Gap.

McClellan's attacks against Turner's Gap were supposed to hold Lee's main body

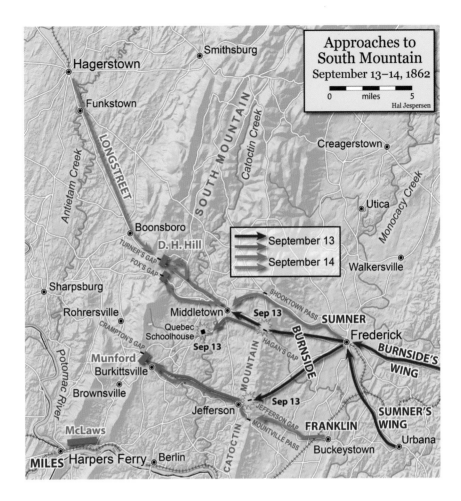

Approaches to
South Mountain
September 13–14, 1862

0      miles      5
Hal Jespersen

September 13
September 14

in place. To the south, William Franklin's Sixth Corps carried the success or failure of McClellan's plan on their shoulders. Like their comrades to the north, Franklin's soldiers awoke early and were soon on the road. They climbed over Catoctin Mountain. The head of the long, 13,000-man column reached Burkittsville at the foot of Crampton's Gap at noon. Franklin took several hours to deploy his corps for the assault of the Confederate defenders at the gap. Punching through the gap was the first part of his objective to relieve Harpers Ferry.

As four columns snaked towards South Mountain from the east and northwest, "Stonewall" Jackson worked to hurry the reduction of Dixon Miles's garrison at Harpers Ferry before it could be relieved. Lee's three columns had accomplished an incredible feat by September 14: all of them had converged on the high ground surrounding the town. McLaws's men manhandled four guns to the crest of Maryland Heights. Walker's men did what Miles deemed impossible: placed five guns atop Loudoun Heights. Twenty-two of Jackson's guns unlimbered west of Bolivar Heights.

Miles's own men saw the Confederate gunners homing in on them. Some Yankee artillerists vainly tried to make the deployment difficult for Walker's cannoneers but the height of the mountain

above the Federal gun positions ensured that few of their shells found their target.

With the ring of guns surrounding Harpers Ferry, Jackson planned to coordinate the bombardment among the three commands. Signal flag transmission was slow, though it was Jackson's best means to communicate his intentions to Walker and McLaws. Finally, at 2:00 p.m., egged on by the Federal fire, the impatient Walker ordered his guns to open fire. The rest of the Confederate guns—29 in all—soon followed suit.

The incoming Confederate fire was accurate. One Federal constantly scampering for safety as shells fell about him

▲ This spectacular view of the Middletown Valley from Mountville Pass greeted William Franklin's Sixth Corps soldiers during their descent into Jefferson on September 14. Crampton's Gap can be seen directly above the large barn in the foreground. (Author's collection)

◄ Named for a small stone schoolhouse located nearby, Schoolhouse Ridge was used by "Stonewall" Jackson's forces as a way to close the trap on the Federals in Harpers Ferry. The ridge parallels the Federal position along Bolivar Heights. (Author's collection)

said the enemy gunners "made it too hot for any troops to stand," let alone the green troops that comprised a sizable portion of the Harpers Ferry garrison. Union gunners tried to respond to the enemy fire and provide encouragement for their own infantry. This fire, however, was ineffective. In some ways so was the Confederate barrage as it caused little physical damage to Miles's men. But the mental toll wore on them. "I tell you, it is dreadful to be a mark for artillery," one New York captain wrote, "bad enough for any but especially for raw troops; it demoralizes them—it rouses one's courage to be able to fight in return, but to sit still and calmly be cut in two is too much to ask."

By the afternoon of September 14, smoke and fire from battle spread down the spine of South Mountain from Frostown Gap to Crampton's Gap, a distance of nearly seven

miles. An additional seven miles south of Crampton's Gap lay Harpers Ferry. Fire engulfed two battlefields on nearly a fifteen-mile front.

Despite the Confederate artillery superiority established around three sides of Harpers Ferry, the Union garrison did not capitulate. The Confederate soldiers on South Mountain fought to protect the rear of McLaws's command in Pleasant Valley and on Maryland Heights, and to buy time for the Harpers Ferry operation to be successfully concluded.

While the reverberations of cannon fire rippled up Pleasant Valley towards Turner's Gap, D. H. Hill worked feverishly directing troops into his defensive line. Hill knew that a good defense sometimes required a good offense, too. With that in mind, Hill cobbled together a force of four brigades to take back control of Fox's Gap and

▼ At the time of the battle, this hillside was clear of trees. This small viewshed gives you an idea of the perspective from here toward the Confederate position on Schoolhouse Ridge. It was near here that Jackson ordered his diversionary attack against the Federal line on September 14. (Author's collection)

drive the Ninth Corps off the mountain. He placed the four brigades—about 4,000 men—under the command of Ohio-born Brigadier General Roswell Ripley. They lined up in the Old Sharpsburg Road facing south. Brigadier General Thomas Drayton's brigade held Fox's Gap itself. Colonel George T. Anderson's brigade formed on his right followed by Ripley's own brigade. Brigadier General George B. Anderson's North Carolinians anchored the right of the line on the mountain's eastern slope.

As troops continued to arrive from Turner's Gap, the brigades on the right of Ripley's line had to slide down the mountain to make room for them. When the battle resumed at Fox's Gap, Ripley's brigades did not connect with one another. The dense woods and broken terrain only exacerbated the Confederate efforts for a coordinated attack against the Ninth Corps.

The advances of both contending forces began about the same time, though Willcox's division had considerably more luck coordinating their movements. Colonel Benjamin Christ's brigade formed north of the Old Sharpsburg Road while Colonel Thomas Welsh's men held the ground south of it. Both brigades faced west up the mountain. At 4:00 p.m., they advanced.

Drayton's Confederates situated in the gap itself found 300 yards between them and G. T. Anderson's brigade on their right. Further complicating the situation, Drayton's brigade faced two different directions. Two Georgia regiments were oriented east while the rest of the brigade deployed in the Old Sharpsburg Road facing south. Drayton sent one company of South Carolinians south across Wise's open field as skirmishers. Those South Carolinians ran into Willcox's opposing skirmish line and saw the weight of Willcox's division behind them.

With no friendly force to his immediate right and with a large enemy force in front of him, Drayton boldly decided to attack rather than wait for the rest of Ripley's attack—which was having its own troubles—to begin. Drayton's men surged south out of the roadbed. Fierce fighting erupted again in Fox's Gap. The Federals still held the upper hand and drove Drayton's men back to the Old Sharpsburg Road, where the Confederates dealt death from behind the stone walls lining the road. Willcox's 45th Pennsylvania lost 21 men killed and 115 wounded in the action.

Federal troops advancing north of the road, the 17th Michigan, drove the eastern-facing Georgia regiments back from their position. Drayton recalled them to his line fronting south to aid against the bulk of Willcox's division. The arrival of more Union soldiers, especially artillery in Sturgis's division, drove Drayton's artillery support from the field, worsening a bad situation for the 1828 West Point graduate. Then, from the south, the 30th Ohio, 46th New York, and 45th Pennsylvania attacked Drayton's right. As the battle roared, the 17th Michigan struck Drayton's exposed left and rear, completing the rout of the Confederate brigade from the field.

Drayton faced Willcox alone. His men fought as hard as could be expected of them in their perilous circumstance. They paid for their solo fight against larger numbers. As a whole, the brigade, which went into the fight with 1,300 men, counted 206 men killed, 227 wounded, and 210 missing for their total casualty count of 643, half the brigade. The 3rd South Carolina Battalion exited the fight with only 24 of its 160 men unscathed. The 50th and 51st Georgia held Drayton's left during the action; the former regiment lost more than 75 percent of its men while the latter lost 60 percent.

found the guns of Captain Joseph Clark's Regular battery and tried to take them. As they advanced, Colonel Harrison Fairchild's recently arrived brigade of New Yorkers from Brigadier General Isaac Rodman's division supported Clark's gunners and helped beat back Anderson's attack.

Back at the gap, Sturgis settled his Union lines. He sent skirmishers north to determine the enemy positions. At this moment, with the sun setting and light lessening, Ninth Corps commander Maj. Gen. Jesse Reno rode into Fox's Gap. Reno had been with army commander McClellan and wing commander Burnside but hurried to his corps' positions once it seemed that their advance stalled. He rode to spur them forward. While watching another Federal reconnaissance probe north, Hood's concealed men opened a scattering fire. One bullet hit Reno just below the heart; he soon died. Reno became one of the last soldiers to fall at Fox's Gap.

The Ninth Corps' afternoon advance was part of a double envelopment planned by Burnside to take Turner's Gap from the north and south rather than taking it directly along the National Road. The fight for the principal gap in South Mountain erupted on a three-mile front. While Reno's men battled for Fox's Gap, Maj. Gen. Joseph Hooker's First Corps troops fought over difficult ground at Turner's and Frostown gaps.

Hooker's men began marching from their camps east of Frederick before daybreak. After marching about 15 miles, they approached the foot of South Mountain at 2:30 p.m.

Hooker quickly looked at the tough assignment he and his men received, and he went to work preparing them to take the important ground north of Turner's Gap. Under artillery cover, Brigadier General George Meade's Pennsylvania Reserve

More soldiers from both armies made their way to Fox's Gap. After the rout of Drayton's brigade, Brigadier General Samuel Sturgis's men relieved Willcox's embattled division. John Hood's division also arrived and took a position north of the gap after a long march from Hagerstown.

Roswell Ripley tried to lend Drayton's brigade support when he heard the shooting start. The mountainous terrain and thick vegetation were Ripley's greatest enemies. His three remaining brigades attempted to sweep south and drive the enemy back. Instead, they lost touch with one another, marched in opposite directions and across each other's front, and had no bearing on the outcome of the fighting.

George B. Anderson's brigade made their way to the Federal left flank. There, they division formed their battle lines. One and a half miles north of the National Road, Brigadier General Truman Seymour's brigade held Meade's right. Colonel Thomas Gallagher's brigade centered Meade's line while Colonel Albert Magilton's brigade completed Meade's deployment. Magilton's left rested on modern-day Dahlgren Road.

On Meade's left, Hooker ordered Brigadier General John Hatch's division to array its battle formation. Rather than one long line like Meade's division assumed, Hatch stacked his three brigades—2,400 men total—one behind the other two hundred yards apart. Brigadier General Marsena Patrick's New Yorkers occupied the front line. Colonel Walter Phelps, Jr.'s brigade backed up Patrick while Brigadier General Abner Doubleday's men brought up the rear. Hooker placed Brigadier General James Ricketts's division as the corps' reserve.

Along the National Road, Burnside ordered Hooker to leave one brigade behind. This lot fell to Brigadier General John Gibbon's all-Western Black Hat Brigade. Gibbon's assignment on the National Road was "for the purpose of making a demonstration upon the enemy's center, up the main pike, as soon as the movements of Generals Hooker and Reno had sufficiently progressed," reported Burnside. Near 5:00 p.m., Hooker's 12,000 men formed a line that stretched nearly one and a half miles.

▲ The Reno Monument was one of the first monuments erected on a Maryland Campaign battlefield. It dates to 1889 and is supposed to mark the exact location of Reno's mortal wounding but, in reality, it stands about 200 yards from that spot. (Author's collection)

▶ During the advance against Turner's Gap, a bullet slammed into John Hatch's right leg, knocking him out of field command for the remainder of the war. In 1893, he received the Medal of Honor for his actions at South Mountain. (Library of Congress)

From the mountaintop, D. H. Hill watched the numbers tip further in the Federals' favor. The Army of the Potomac's "marching columns extended back as far as the eye could see," he later wrote. Hill prepared his meager force for the worst.

At the start of the day, only Colquitt's brigade astride the National Road stood between McClellan's vast columns and Turner's Gap. At noon, Brigadier General Robert Rodes's Alabama brigade reached the gap alongside Ripley's southward-destined men. Rodes, under Hill's direction, placed his men on Colquitt's left. As Hooker's corps marched north beyond Rodes's left, the Alabamans received orders to move three quarters of a mile further north, creating a wide gap in Hill's line

directly protecting Turner's Gap. Rodes's five Alabama regiments failed to connect with each other due to the space the brigade covered and the mountain's broken terrain, woodlots, and ravines.

The hearts of Rodes's men sank as they watched Meade's division deploy in front of them. Behind them, some support arrived in the form of Brigadier General Nathan Evans' brigade, commanded directly by Col. Peter Stevens. They were strung out in their battleline to Rodes's right across Dahlgren Road.

While numbers rested in the Federals' favor, terrain favored Hill's Confederates. "All up the mountain side rocks and boulders abound, and here and there, stone walls," wrote one of Meade's Pennsylvanians. "When to these features are added the heavily wooded portions and frequent depressions in the ground itself, some idea may be gathered of the difficulty of the task laid upon the division." With this difficulty readily apparent in their front, Meade's soldiers gripped their rifles tighter, checked their equipment, and prepared for battle.

At 5:00 p.m., Hooker launched his corps up the mountain. Obstinate skirmishing broke into a pitched battle between Rodes's and Seymour's commands. The weight of Federal numbers told and the bluecoats drifted up the mountain, hardly maintaining the formations they held at the beginning of the attack.

Rodes shifted his leftmost regiment, Col. John Gordon's 6th Alabama, further left to hold onto a spur on the mountain's eastern slope. Gordon's men fought valiantly but could not stem the blue tide. As Seymour pressured Rodes's left, Gallagher's and Magilton's brigades struck his front. Confederate fire and difficult terrain broke up Meade's line, but only temporarily. Pennsylvanian grit met Alabama determination and won. Rodes's

▼ Robert Rodes's Alabama Brigade lost 422 out of the 1,200 men it carried into action north of Turner's Gap. D. H. Hill wrote of Rodes's performance in his after-action report that he "handled his little brigade in a most admirable and gallant manner, fighting, for hours, vastly superior odds, and maintaining the key-points of the position until darkness rendered a further advance of the Yankees impossible." (National Park Service)

Alabamans fled up the mountain and clung to a position near the mountain's summit until darkness relieved the Alabama troops.

Peter Stevens's South Carolinians likewise shattered Magilton's battle line with volleys of lead. The Federals gathered themselves, regrouped, and continued the uphill climb. In the end, Confederate volleys only slowed Meade's attack, but did not stop it. Darkness, fatigue, and a shortage of ammunition ended the fighting for Frostown Gap.

Despite the Confederates' superior defensive position, Meade's 4,000 men suffered fewer casualties—392—than the enemy they faced. Rodes's 1,200 men lost one-third of their fighting strength; Stevens's brigade, which began the fight 550 men strong, was reduced by approximately 40 percent.

John Hatch's division had an equally difficult task on Meade's left. Fixed in three battle lines, Hatch's advance occurred simultaneously with Meade's. The few Confederates that stood in Hatch's way panted after a long march from Hagerstown that ended atop South Mountain. They deployed near the summit of a spur that hung from South Mountain's eastern slope.

Initially sent south to Fox's Gap, the three brigades of brigadier generals James Kemper and Richard Garnett and Colonel Joseph Walker reached Turner's Gap just as Hooker's assault commenced. Maj. Gen. James Longstreet, now in command of the Confederate side of the field, sent the exhausted brigades up Dahlgren Road. Kemper's men faced northeast, Garnett east, and Walker's men deployed behind Garnett's right.

No sooner did these approximately 1,500 Confederates send skirmishers to their front than firing began between them and Hatch's advanced pickets. Two regiments of Marsena Patrick's brigade led Hatch's men onto the field. The terrain quickly split the

▲ The Haupt (background) and O'Neil (foreground) farms stood in the assault path of the Pennsylvania Reserves, who attacked from right to left. Rodes's Alabama brigade disputed them from around these two homes. (Author's collection)

regiments and sent them in two different directions. Patrick tried to sort out the mess. In the process, Phelps's line passed through and beyond the former front line. There, they found the main enemy line.

Safely hugging a formidable stone wall, Garnett's men staggered Phelps's advance. The Federals broke ranks to seek whatever shelter the mountain provided and brawled with Garnett's line for the next fifteen minutes. Supported by Patrick's reformed regiments, Hatch's two lead brigades charged and drove back Kemper's brigade, which lost close to 20 percent of its numbers.

Garnett's men aimed and fired in the enemy's faces to no effect. The Union battleline "never paused nor faltered." Instead, it rushed forward and drove Garnett from the summit of the spur where he had staged his line. The stand cost Garnett's Virginians 196 of the 400 men it went into battle with. Phelps's attack claimed 95 of his 400 men.

In the growing darkness, Hatch pushed his rear line, Doubleday's brigade, into the fight and suffered a wound in the process. Doubleday leapfrogged to division command while Colonel William Wainwright assumed the brigade vacancy. The command changes hardly slowed Wainwright's men, who pitched into the remnants of Garnett's brigade and Col. Joseph Walker's advancing Confederates. Walker's arrival on the firing line stunned and temporarily broke Wainwright's line, but the Yankees soon rallied, and the two opposing formations traded gunfire at point blank range in the increasing darkness. Elements of Ricketts's division reached the front to relieve Hatch's men, who by this point were reaching into empty cartridge boxes. The men under Ricketts's command did not budge; Longstreet's three brigades withdrew closer to Turner's Gap.

Walker's losses totaled just 32 men as much of the fight took place in the smoky dusk. Hatch's three brigades and Ricketts's lone engaged unit—Brigadier General George Hartsuff's brigade—tallied 194 casualties of their own.

Between the two pincers of the Ninth and First corps, Brig. Gen. John Gibbon's Western brigade—the Black Hats—operated

▶ Brigadier General John Hatch's division attacked in the open fields leading up to South Mountain. After Hatch was wounded, he was taken to the Daniel Sheffer farm, which can be seen on the left side of the photograph. (Author's collection)

as a diversionary force against Colquitt's line, the Confederate center, astride the National Road near the bottom of the mountain east of Turner's Gap. Burnside intended for Gibbon's four regiments to attract the Confederate center's attention until Reno's and Hooker's attacks "had sufficiently progressed." At that time, around 5:00 p.m., Burnside ordered Gibbon's brigade into the teeth of Turner's Gap itself.

Supported by friendly artillery behind them and opposed by enemy fire for two hours while they waited, Gibbon's brigade finally received the command, "Forward." The brigade straddled the National Road and ran into Colquitt's 1,300 men strongly positioned behind a stone wall not far up the mountain. One of Gibbon's staffers succinctly called Colquitt's defenses "an ugly place to attack."

On the south side of the road, the 19th Indiana and 2nd Wisconsin drove Colquitt's skirmishers back. Then, the 2nd Wisconsin saw its sister Badger State regiments come under a severe enfilading fire. From south of the road, this regiment lent its leaden weight to the battle raging north of the pike.

There, the 6th and 7th Wisconsin battled in the waning daylight and attempted to outflank Colquitt's line. In the end, all they could do too was drive in the enemy skirmishers and cling to the little ground they won. Colquitt's Georgians and Alabamans made them pay dearly for it. At a cost of 10 percent of its strength, Colquitt's infantry inflicted 318 casualties on Gibbon's brigade, or roughly 25 percent of the men who began the attack. Heroes and nicknames were born of the fight along the National Road. Alfred Colquitt became known as the "The Rock of South Mountain." Gibbon's brigade went down in history as the Iron Brigade.

Meanwhile, six miles south of Turner's Gap, Union and Confederate soldiers battled for possession of Crampton's Gap. Once he reached the foot of South Mountain, Sixth Corps commander Maj. Gen. William Franklin paused to reconnoiter the enemy position and rest his command after a march of over ten miles.

◀ One member of Hooker's corps had a similar view of South Mountain from its base and remembered afterwards, "It looked like a task to storm." Gibbon's brigade attacked directly into Turner's Gap along both sides of the National Road. (Author's collection)

Locals told Sixth Corps soldiers that the Confederate defenders west of Burkittsville numbered 4,000 infantry, hundreds of cavalrymen, and a couple guns. McClellan reminded Franklin, "Continue to bear in mind the necessity of relieving Colonel Miles if possible."

Franklin's enemy, Maj. Gen. Lafayette McLaws, was intent on preventing such a junction of Franklin's and Miles's forces. McLaws was as equally stunned by the rapidity of the Army of the Potomac's movements as the rest of the Confederate high command. Thus, his men mostly aligned south, facing Harpers Ferry, not north facing Franklin. The only Confederates guarding Crampton's Gap by midday on September 14 were 800 infantry and cavalry and a few guns headed by Colonel Thomas Munford positioned along the eastern foot of South Mountain. Brigadier General Paul Semmes led an additional 300 men at Brownsville Pass one mile south, another potential route for a Union move into Pleasant Valley.

The morning sun revealed Franklin's force moving towards South Mountain. Semmes and Munford immediately called for help. McLaws responded by sending Brigadier General Howell Cobb's 1,350-man brigade to Brownsville where it could support either gap that Franklin might punch through.

By 3:00 p.m., Franklin began deploying his corps for an attack against Crampton's Gap. Major General Henry Slocum

▲ John Gibbon's brigade suffered 318 casualties while storming Turner's Gap. Its performance on September 14 earned them the nickname "Iron Brigade" in popular memory, though at least two other brigades claimed that same title in the Army of the Potomac. (Library of Congress)

◄ Maj. Gen. Lafayette McLaws was a rising star in the Army of Northern Virginia by the time of the Maryland Campaign. Many historians believe Lee was grooming him for a possible corps or wing command. (Library of Congress)

received the assignment and fanned out his three brigades north of Burkittsville. The division's brigades stacked in three lines one behind the other. Colonel Joseph Bartlett's led the way. Brigadier General John Newton's brigade formed in two lines behind Bartlett while Colonel Alfred Torbert's New Jerseyans deployed in the same formation behind Newton. Counting Bartlett's skirmishers, the division stood six lines deep, each line separated by 150–200 yards. The outnumbered Confederates watched from their line along Mountain Church Road and were in awe "at the magnificent splendor of the martial army that was slowly and steadily moving toward us across the plain below like a living

▲ Crampton's Gap is the low notch in South Mountain in this view looking from William Franklin's headquarters east of Burkittsville. (Author's collection)

▶ Henry Slocum's division led the assault against Crampton's Gap. By the end of the war, Slocum rose to command of the Army of Georgia during William T. Sherman's march through the Carolinas. (Library of Congress)

One Federal soldier described the attack across fields towards Crampton's Gap as through corn, over stubblefields and meadows, separated from each other by stone and zig-zag fences and potted with thickets, stone piles, rocks, gullies, and quagmires." He also deemed the enemy position along Mountain Church Road "one of the strongest and, naturally, most defensible positions held by either party during the war, and one of the most difficult to surmount." (Author's collection)

panorama," said one Southern artillerist. At 4:00 p.m., Bartlett's skirmishers advanced and engaged Munford's thin line.

Despite having fewer men, the Confederate defenders poured well-aimed shots of artillery and musketry into Bartlett's line, forcing him to relieve his skirmishers. Volleying continued back and forth for the two sides and the Federals seemed to get the worst of what one regimental commander called "a severe and galling fire."

After an hour of slugging it out with Munford's men, Bartlett's soldiers began running low on ammunition. Bartlett called for help from Newton's brigade. In the advance, the two brigades became separated, which meant Bartlett's men remained on the firing line for an unusually long amount of time before Newton's troops relieved them.

◄ Col. Joseph Jackson Bartlett was a lawyer in southern New York when the Civil War broke out. His superiors recommended him for a brigadier general's commission for his stellar performance in front of Crampton's Gap. Bartlett named the horse he rode on September 14, 1862 "Crampton" for the gap his men helped seize. (Library of Congress)

Newton brought the full weight of his brigade onto the front line. Torbert's New Jerseyans soon extended his left while the 96th Pennsylvania, part of Bartlett's brigade, arrived on the division's right. Firepower was the tool Slocum relied on to seize the gap, but the Federal fire was "ineffectual" against Munford's command behind that stone wall. Slocum brought artillery into the fight and Franklin sent Brigadier General William Brooks's Vermont brigade south of Burkittsville to protect Slocum's left and look for an opportunity on that end of the enemy line.

Incredibly, the Confederate line still held. Audible cheers from the gap indicated Confederate reinforcements had arrived. Bartlett determined, "It became apparent to all that nothing but a united charge would dislodge the enemy and win the battle." Torbert agreed. The two men rode along their line preparing their men for a charge. Brooks ordered his men to charge too. The united Federal line surged forward at 5:20 p.m.

The coordinated charge of the four Union brigades finally cracked Munford's line. The Confederates held on until the last second, many of them delivering a close-range volley before fleeing up the mountain. Brief hand-to-hand fighting occurred on the Confederate left but the 96th Pennsylvania prevailed there. Up the steep mountain slope the Confederates went with Union infantry close behind them.

Munford's men ran into new Confederate formations in their rear, namely the 16th Georgia and Cobb's Legion of Howell Cobb's recently arrived brigade. Cobb placed his other two regiments nearer the gap while these two deployed on the mountain side. Soon after the bolting Confederates ran through his lines, Cobb's two regiments had to face the enemy. The overwhelming pursuit and the confusing

terrain led Cobb's Legion to be hit on three sides. Of 250 men carried into the fight, 33 were killed or wounded and 156 became prisoners. Cobb's line ran for the rear.

With a flag in his hand, Cobb tried to patch together another defensive line in Crampton's Gap itself with two guns and whatever infantry he could scrape together. It only temporarily slowed the Federal onslaught. By 6:45 p.m., over 30 minutes after sunset, Franklin's corps secured the gap.

Confederate troops tallied approximately 1,000 losses, more than 60 percent of whom were prisoners. The Sixth Corps lost 533 men.

▲ Alfred Thomas Archimedes Torbert's men charged into Crampton's Gap with an axe to grind—especially the 4th New Jersey, which had almost entirely surrendered to the enemy at Gaines's Mill on June 27, 1862. "Remember the 27th of June!" yelled their colonel, William Hatch, as his New Jerseyans went into the fight. (Library of Congress)

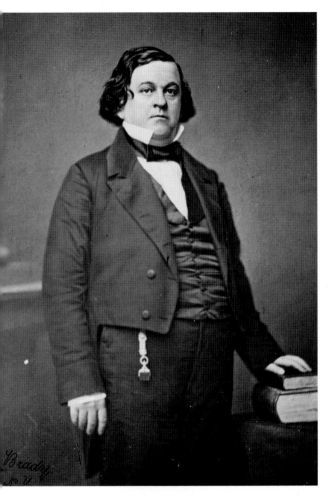

Franklin's men had more work to do though. He pushed some of them down the western slope of the mountain for tomorrow's work of relieving Harpers Ferry.

In Pleasant Valley, the Union piercing of South Mountain compelled McLaws to turn his focus away from Harpers Ferry and instead worry about his rear. He stripped most of his forces encircling Dixon Miles's garrison and stretched them in a line across Pleasant Valley one mile south of Crampton's Gap. By the next morning, McLaws's line studded 27 guns and 4,400 infantry to oppose Franklin. That line and darkness stopped any Union advance on September 14.

That evening, Robert E. Lee, who due to his injuries had been unable to personally

◀ Howell Cobb's brigade suffered heavily in its short but sharp fight at Crampton's Gap, losing 495 soldiers—nearly 40 percent of the brigade's strength. Before the war, Cobb served as a United States congressman, Speaker of the House, and Secretary of the Treasury before pledging allegiance to the Confederacy. His superior officers pinned much of the blame over what happened at Crampton's Gap on Cobb despite the difficult situation forced upon him when he arrived on the field. (Library of Congress)

► Confederates fled from the base of South Mountain into Crampton's Gap using Whipp's Ravine. Their Union pursuers utilized the same terrain feature to bring them into Crampton's Gap and secure the gap for the Army of the Potomac. (Author's collection)

◄ Civil War correspondent George Alfred Townsend, who often wrote with the penname "Gath," memorialized 157 war correspondents with this 50-foot-tall arch at the top of Crampton's Gap. The monument was completed in 1896. (Author's collection)

direct or view the fighting around Turner's Gap, met with his subordinates, chiefly James Longstreet and D. H. Hill. Neither general gave Lee encouraging news. Hill "explained that the enemy was in great force with commanding positions on both flanks," Longstreet remembered. Lee could not remain at South Mountain. Quickly, couriers darted from his headquarters carrying orders for a Confederate withdrawal from Turner's and Fox's gaps.

Lee's decision to delay McClellan to buy time for Jackson to force Harpers Ferry's surrender had failed. He could not forget about McLaws's two divisions in Pleasant Valley, either, though he did not have good news to relay to McLaws. "The day has gone against us," Lee told McLaws, "and this army will go by Sharpsburg and cross the river" into Virginia. "It is necessary for you to abandon your position tonight," said Lee.

After only ten days in Maryland, Lee himself threw up the white flag on his campaign that began with so much promise.

# Roads to Antietam

Robert E. Lee decided to reunite his disparate army and resurrect his campaign north of the Potomac River by making a stand west of Antietam Creek. On September 15–16, 1862, thousands of soldiers from both armies converged on the crossroads town of Sharpsburg.

Union soldiers in Col. Dixon Miles's garrison huddled for cover from the raining Confederate artillery shells throughout the afternoon of September 14, 1862. They were trapped in a ring of fire but still held out against "Stonewall" Jackson's commands towering above them and carefully aiming shot and shell into the Federal masses.

Jackson's artillery barrage was impressive and deadly. But since it still failed to bring about the garrison's capitulation—and knowing he needed a quick end to the stalemate at Harpers Ferry—Jackson turned to his infantry. Storming Bolivar Heights carried few prospects of success, so Jackson ordered the divisions of brigadier generals Alexander Lawton and John R. Jones to demonstrate in front of the main Federal line. Thus distracted, the Confederate commander hoped Miles and his men would miss Major General A. P. Hill's division marching around the Federal left to seize ground between the Union line on Bolivar Heights and the Shenandoah River.

▶ Remains of the bolts holding the pontoon bridges that once spanned the Potomac River at Harpers Ferry during the Civil War still remain—a small reminder of the past. (Library of Congress)

Under artillery cover, Jackson's demonstration commenced. Hill's men quietly marched along the river bank. Before dusk, they seized their objective and ended the day within 150 yards of Miles's troops. Hill believed "the fate of Harper's Ferry was sealed."

Hill's optimism infected Jackson. He scribbled off a note of hope to Robert E. Lee. Jackson recognized God's divine hand in the movement and prayed for "complete success tomorrow." The rider carrying the note raced off into the darkness looking for army headquarters.

Though Hill's move checkmated Miles's soldiers, not all of them were trapped in Jackson's cage. Southern-born Colonel Benjamin "Grimes" Davis would not let his cavalrymen and horses become Jackson's prisoners. At 7:00 p.m. on the 14th, Davis and other cavalry officers proceeded to Miles's headquarters. Their cavalry was no use, they argued. Miles eventually consented to let the 1,500 troopers in the garrison attempt a breakout and gave Colonel Arno Voss the command, though Davis still factored largely into the column's ride.

The troopers silently spurred their horses into column. Miles wished them luck and ordered Voss "to force his way through the enemy's line and join our army." At 8:00 p.m., the column began riding across the pontoon bridge spanning the Potomac River into Maryland. Few Confederate pickets guarded the bridge (most had been pulled into McLaws's Pleasant Valley line) but some scattered shots rang out on the Maryland shore when part of the Federal column took a wrong turn. They corrected themselves and rejoined the rest of the column.

In the inky black of the night, Voss's troopers felt their way along Maryland's roads and fields. Four hours after their ride started, the van of the column reached Sharpsburg. In the town's main street, the cavalrymen briefly clashed with the head of Lee's army as it made its way towards the Potomac River. The cavalry disengaged and continued their ride north.

Several more hours of riding brought the troopers to the outskirts of Williamsport. By chance, about 5:00 a.m. on September 15, they met the reserve ammunition wagon train of Longstreet's command and

◄ These 20 cannons beyond the left flank of Miles' line on Bolivar Heights were critical in forcing the surrender of the Union garrison on the morning of September 15. Bolivar Heights can be seen in the distance above the third gun from the left. (Author's collection)

captured between 72 and 104 of the wagons and 100 prisoners.

With their prizes in tow, the column's head arrived in Greencastle, Pennsylvania, at 9:00 a.m. Federal losses totaled 178 men were missing when they counted at Greencastle. Voss, greatly helped by Davis, led the column approximately 50 miles and brought the cavalry out of the gloomy situation at Harpers Ferry.

The cavalry was lucky to get out when it did. Fog concealed the morning sun at Harpers Ferry on the morning of September 15. A breeze and the rising sun slowly dissipated the fog and revealed that the Federals' already perilous position had worsened. A. P. Hill's infantry was on the left flank of Bolivar Heights along with five artillery batteries his men had manhandled into position during the night. Additionally, Jackson's artillery chief, Colonel Stapleton Crutchfield, had brought ten guns across the Shenandoah River to a shelf on Loudoun Heights from where they could hit the reverse side of Bolivar Heights. With

their pieces sited, Confederate artillerists began pounding the Yankee positions once the fog disappeared.

After the artillery duel of the previous day, Miles's artillerists were almost out of ammunition. The garrison could not hold out for long under the punishing, concentric fire of nearly 50 Confederate guns. For an hour, they tried. Miles called together his subordinates to discuss their situation. The council agreed to surrender.

White flags, handkerchiefs, and rags—anything that might get the enemy to stop shooting—popped up among the Union lines. Miles himself joined in, riding among the troops. It took time for distant Confederates to see the surrender signals; some batteries continued firing. One of the last shells exploded near Miles. Shrapnel tore the flesh off Miles's left calf. He died the next day while his garrison surrendered.

Julius White handled the surrender proceedings. Harpers Ferry's capture by the Confederates netted them 73 cannons, 11,000 small arms, 200 wagons, and 12,400

▶ Miles had his headquarters here during his time at Harpers Ferry. He was brought back here after his mortal wounding and died here. Today, the building is an information center for Harpers Ferry National Historical Park. (Author's collection)

## Profile:
## Major General Thomas "Stonewall" Jackson, 1824–63

Born on January 21, 1824, in what is now West Virginia, Thomas Jackson was orphaned as a young boy following the deaths of his parents. Despite his humble upbringing, Jackson became a member of the United States Military Academy's estimable Class of 1846. This class produced 24 future Civil War generals, including David R. Jones, George B. McClellan, Jesse Reno, Truman Seymour, and Samuel Sturgis. Jackson graduated seventeenth out of 59 cadets, placing him in the artillery branch of the United States Army. Like many of his classmates, Jackson fought in the Mexican-American War and earned praise for his performance under fire. In peacetime, Jackson accused his commanding officer, Maj. William French, of having an affair and was arrested. Simultaneously, an offer for Jackson to teach at the Virginia Military Institute (VMI) arrived. Jackson resigned his army commission and moved to Lexington, Virginia, to begin his new role at VMI. He taught there until the Civil War began in 1861. His cadets helped drill and train the flood of recruits enlisting in Confederate service at the beginning of the conflict. Jackson's ability as a commanding officer became apparent by the conduct of his Virginia brigade on Henry House Hill during the battle of First Manassas. There, Jackson and his brigade received their immortal nicknames, "Stonewall." Jackson took command in the Shenandoah Valley in the fall of 1861. The next spring, he led a successful campaign there against three separate Union forces to prevent Federal reinforcements from supporting the Army of the Potomac on the Virginia Peninsula. When Robert E. Lee took command of the Army of Northern Virginia, Jackson's command was called east and participated in the Seven Days Campaign. Jackson's penchant for marching his troops was put to good use when he marched his half of the army around the Army of Virginia and cut its supply line during the Second Manassas Campaign. His men then blunted multiple enemy attacks during the battle of Second Manassas. Jackson successfully, though belatedly, forced Harpers Ferry's garrison to surrender during the Maryland Campaign. At Fredericksburg, his men fought off an enemy breakthrough. The next spring at the battle of Chancellorsville, Jackson led a march around the Union right flank and crushed it. He was wounded that night while reconnoitering in front of his lines and died from disease he developed while recuperating on May 10, 1863.

▲ Thomas "Stonewall" Jackson. (Library of Congress)

Federal prisoners who signed paroles and were out of the war until exchanged. For what they netted, the six Confederate divisions suffered light casualties: 39 killed and 247 wounded. Miles's garrison lost 44 men killed and 173 wounded—mostly in the fighting on Maryland Heights—before the shooting stopped.

Jackson wrote a note to Lee and hurried it to the army commander. "Through God's blessing," the pious Jackson wrote, "Harper's Ferry and its garrison are to be surrendered." Robert E. Lee received this message while on an eminence east of Sharpsburg overlooking Antietam Creek.

Following a night of pulling his soldiers away from Turner's and Fox's gaps and declaring his stay in Maryland over, a wearied, worn-out, injured Lee exited the ambulance that bore him from the base of South Mountain to Keedysville on the east side of Antietam Creek. There, Lee vowed to temporarily pause his army's retreat to give Lafayette McLaws's boxed-in divisions a chance to "more readily join us," said Lee. The general made this slight change

in his plans after learning of McLaws's fate following the fall of Crampton's Gap.

From Keedysville, the forces directly with Lee could strike the Federal flank should McClellan turn his columns south into Pleasant Valley to crush McLaws. The safety of McLaws's command was paramount in Lee's mind.

As the general disembarked from the rickety ambulance to stretch his legs before sunrise on September 15, information brought to him indicated that the ground at Keedysville was less defensible than the high ground on the west side of Antietam Creek outside Sharpsburg. He ordered his army there to protect McLaws.

Before Lee re-entered the ambulance that would carry him three miles to the high ground around Sharpsburg, optimism brightened Lee's demeanor, which came from a courier bearing Jackson's message of the previous night predicting Harpers Ferry's collapse. Maybe Lee could still resurrect his campaign.

Once Lee reached the high ground east of Sharpsburg behind Antietam Creek, he

▼ Both Robert E. Lee and George B. McClellan had a similar view in September 1862—Lee in the days before the battle and McClellan during the fighting. From near this vantage point, a Northern correspondent examined the Confederate position. It "was a broad table-land of forest and ravine, cover for troops everywhere, nowhere easy access for an enemy ... It was all a Rebel stronghold beyond." Cemetery Hill is in the right center of the photograph just above the tree line. (Author's collection)

▲ In 1862, Sharpsburg was on the verge of celebrating the centennial anniversary of its founding in 1763. Approximately 1,300 people called Sharpsburg home in 1860. Many German farmers settled the area. 150 slaves and 203 free Blacks lived in Sharpsburg in the year prior to the beginning of the Civil War. Sharpsburg suffered extensive damage during the battle of Antietam as the two armies battled through the fields adjoining the town. (Library of Congress)

◄ Warned of an impending battle, the civilians of Sharpsburg fled the town in droves. "Many of the inhabitants ... terror stricken fled from the town to the country, carrying with them a few articles of clothing," recalled young resident John P. Smith. Some sought shelter at Killiansburg Cave along the Potomac River while others escaped to neighboring communities. (Library of Congress)

began fanning his brigades and batteries along a ridgeline—Sharpsburg Heights—that ran over two miles north, east, and south of Sharpsburg. A local civilian heard Lee discussing the situation with Maj. Gen. James Longstreet, saying they did not intend to keep their army at Sharpsburg permanently, "although they admitted it was the most splendid position they could possibly have."

Lee's assessment of the terrain was correct. Antietam Creek in his front gave his enemy a natural barrier that it had to cross to engage Lee in pitched battle. The creek was enough of a barrier that troops could only cross at certain points. In the vicinity of the future Antietam battlefield, there were five major crossing points north to south: the Upper Bridge, Pry's Ford one-half mile south, the Middle Bridge that carried the Boonsboro Pike across the creek a little over one mile south of the ford, the Lower Bridge (that became known as Burnside Bridge) another mile further south, and Snavely's Ford one more mile beyond the Lower Bridge. Since McClellan could only cross at a few points, Lee could concentrate portions of his force against McClellan and even the odds.

The high ground that Lee perched his artillery and infantry atop of was equally advantageous. From each of the three bridge crossings, any Federal attacks would have to climb over 180 feet of elevation to reach Lee's main line. Additionally, from east of the creek, Lee was gifted something few commanders received in the Civil War: he saw what McClellan's vantage point would be of the Confederate line. Most importantly, Lee saw that McClellan would not be able to see what was behind Sharpsburg Heights. Lee could use the reverse slope to hide his strength—or lack thereof—and move his columns out of the enemy's view.

## Antietam Creek

Antietam Creek derives its name from an Algonquian phrase that means "swift-flowing stream." The creek originates in Pennsylvania and flows 42 miles to the Potomac River. It served as an obstacle for advancing Federal troops during the battle of Antietam. The creek was about waist deep on the day of the battle, thus making the five passable bridges and fords crucial pieces of the battlefield. Deep water was not the only feature of the creek that prevented Federals from crossing it anywhere. Steep banks and excellently sighted Confederate artillery and infantrymen made the creek a barrier to the Army of the Potomac.

Sharpsburg sat at the convergence of two major roads in the region—the north–south-running Hagerstown Pike and the east–west-running Boonsboro Pike. These roads aided the reunification of Lee's army and provided other benefits. The Hagerstown Pike could carry Lee's army north and allow him to slip by the Federals and continue his campaign of maneuver in Maryland.

The Boonsboro Pike led west toward Boteler's Ford on the Potomac River, Lee's only escape route to Virginia. This was a risk, a position Lee later admitted was "a bad one to hold with the [Potomac] river in rear" just under three miles behind his line. However, there were still several ridges between Sharpsburg Heights and the ford that could serve as fallback positions.

While Lee was placing his army on Sharpsburg Heights, the note from Jackson telling of Harpers Ferry's surrender reached Lee. The army commander ordered Jackson's news announced to the army at Sharpsburg to boost morale. He quickly sent a courier back to Jackson directing him and the divisions at Harpers Ferry—

excepting A. P. Hill's, which was left behind to conclude the surrender proceedings—to join him at Sharpsburg. Lee decided to remain in Maryland and wait for them. He had moved north of the Potomac River to fight and win a battle. He had not won a battle yet, and this could be his chance.

By the end of September 15, Lee's developing line behind Antietam Creek bristled with over a hundred guns supported by approximately 15,000 infantry. Jackson's two divisions, plus those of Walker, McLaws, and Anderson, were on their way from Harpers Ferry. Lee gathered his army together as he watched the Army of the Potomac approach his line.

The battle of South Mountain stripped the Confederates of "the moral effect of our move into Maryland," admitted James Longstreet. The Army of the Potomac experienced the adverse effect. One soldier of Hooker's First Corps noted a morale boost following the battle, and a certain weight lifted off the shoulders of McClellan's troops. "The men felt that if any shadow of discredit had attached to them on account of the disaster at Manassas, it had been swept away by the brilliant flank movement at South Mountain."

Even before Confederate troops began winding their way down the mountain's western slope in retreat, McClellan laid plans to continue the battle the next day or pursue the enemy, whatever situation the morning sun revealed. Edwin Sumner's Second Corps relieved Hooker's troops and the Twelfth Corps rested in Bolivar just behind the Federal battle line. McClellan told Franklin to continue pressing the enemy in front of him in the morning and relieve the Harpers Ferry garrison.

Union pickets crept forward at dawn on September 15 and made it unopposed to the Mountain House in Turner's Gap. The enemy was gone. Aides raced from McClellan's headquarters with pursuit orders. Alfred Pleasonton's cavalry and Israel Richardson's Second Corps division received instructions to advance along the National Road that led down the mountain to Boonsboro backed up by the rest of Sumner's command, Hooker's corps, and the Twelfth Corps. The Ninth Corps, supported by the Fifth Corps, would pursue through Fox's Gap. He ordered his subordinates to move quickly. If they discovered the enemy standing in front of them, "you will dispose your men for attack and report for further orders to the commanding general" so McClellan could consolidate his force against the enemy.

As the corps moved forward, word filtered back to McClellan of a panicked Confederate army and the extent of the Union victory the day before. "If I can believe one tenth of what is reported," McClellan told his wife, "God has seldom given an army a greater victory than this." From Washington, President Lincoln spurred the general on: "Destroy the rebel army, if possible." Only time would tell if Lincoln's request was possible.

McClellan's pursuers clashed in Boonsboro's streets with the surprised Confederate rear guard under Brigadier General Fitzhugh Lee. The Yankee horsemen scattered Lee's troopers. Richardson's division stepped back onto the road and continued the pursuit towards the Potomac River. Shortly after 3:00 p.m., the van of Richardson's column came to the east bank of Antietam Creek. Joseph Hooker accompanied him. There, Hooker and Richardson got their first glance of Lee's new line.

Peering through his glasses, Hooker overestimated Lee's force in front of him at 30,000 men. He reconnoitered the area while awaiting orders from McClellan. As the van of the army halted, the rest of the column clogged the one direct road from Boonsboro to Sharpsburg, which left the army in no position to engage the enemy. When McClellan reached the front after 5:00 p.m., the lack of a sizable force deployed for battle and the lateness of the day forced him to delay an attack. His army spent the rest of the day consolidating on the creek's east bank.

McClellan's pursuit of Lee's main body failed to bring the enemy to grips on September 15. That chase was one part of his plan. William Franklin in Pleasant Valley was the other piece. Franklin's Sixth Corps cautiously probed forward to examine McLaws's line stretched across the valley floor. At 10 a.m., the Confederates received word of Harpers Ferry's surrender and cheered the good news.

While the opposing lines stared down one another, Franklin also overestimated the force in his front. "They outnumber me two to one," he wrote his superior, a fact that steered him away from attacking them. Not wanting a large enemy force on his flank to go unwatched, McClellan ordered Franklin to hold his position in Pleasant Valley.

A heavy fog obscured the Antietam valley on the morning of September 16, preventing each army from viewing the other's position. Perhaps Lee had retreated across the Potomac? One small reconnaissance across the Middle Bridge netted a Confederate prisoner, who informed his Union captors that the Confederate line was still in place on the Sharpsburg Heights. McClellan telegraphed Halleck vowing to "attack as soon as situation of the enemy is developed."

The first task accomplished by McClellan's army that morning was to place "our guns of position." Artillery chief Brigadier General Henry Hunt brought the batteries to a prominent ridge east of the creek. By the morning of September 17,

46 powerful guns crowned the ridge; their two-mile range could reach most of the Confederate line on the opposite side of the creek.

The rest of the morning, both armies continued positioning themselves for the coming fight. More of the Army of Northern Virginia arrived at Sharpsburg that morning—Jackson's two divisions under brigadier generals J. R. Jones and Alexander Lawton as well as John Walker's division. Lee could now count about 26,000 soldiers with him at Sharpsburg with three more divisions on the way from Harpers Ferry. Artillery duels continued across

▼ Henry Hunt had a momentous task organizing the Army of the Potomac's artillery on its march through Maryland. He reported that he "was compelled to obtain on the roads the names and condition of the batteries and the troops to which they were attached." (Library of Congress)

Antietam Creek throughout the morning between the two armies.

Cannon booms and the presence of Lee's army on Sharpsburg Heights revealed as the fog burned off showed McClellan that the task of driving Lee out of Maryland was not yet accomplished. Throughout the morning, McClellan brought more of his infantry corps to the east bank of Antietam Creek. He rode his lines, placed his men, and reconnoitered the enemy positions while contemplating his battle plan. A great unknown in McClellan's mind was the location of Confederate troops from Harpers Ferry. He ordered the Ninth Corps, nominally under Maj. Gen. Ambrose Burnside but tactically led by Brig. Gen. Jacob Cox, to the army's left to protect against—or launch—a potential assault in that sector. These troops lingered near the Lower Bridge, prepared to cross it when ordered to do so.

Union forces controlled three of the five crossing points over Antietam Creek on September 16 (Confederates secured the Lower Bridge and Snavely's Ford). The entire Army of the Potomac could not cross the creek at once. But the northern crossings and Lee's left offered McClellan the best options for chasing the enemy back to Virginia.

McClellan turned to Joseph Hooker's First Corps to be the first Federals to cross Antietam Creek in force. The northern crossings of the creek were open and positioning troops in that sector of the battlefield would both threaten Lee's flank and prevent the Confederate army from moving north on the Hagerstown Pike.

Thus, McClellan's plan "was to make the main attack upon the enemy's left." Then, use the Ninth Corps on his own left "at least to create a diversion in favor of the main attack, with the hope of something more by assailing the enemy's right." If either the main attack was successful or Burnside's diversion was converted to an assault and also met with success, McClellan would use whatever troops he had "on hand" to strike Lee's center along the Boonsboro Pike. This

▼ Philip and Elizabeth Pry suffered terribly because of the battle. Their house was Joseph Hooker's headquarters, George McClellan's command post, and the death place of Israel Richardson. The Prys' well-standing economic status plummeted after the battle, and they moved to Tennessee in 1874 to try and start a new life. (Library of Congress)

plan, if carried out with success, would be enough, McClellan hoped, to hem Lee in between the Army of the Potomac and the Potomac River, forcing Lee to withdraw to Virginia.

At 2:00 p.m., Hooker received orders to march his 9,500 soldiers across Antietam Creek. The movement began two hours later. McClellan promised to send Hooker reinforcements if he needed them and that Hooker would command them once in his vicinity. His objective was to move west from the creek and "to gain the high ground or divide between the Potomac and Antietam Rivers, and then incline to the left, following the elevation toward the left of the rebel army," Hooker remembered. He should not move so far west, McClellan warned, to be out of range of the supporting guns of position.

Meade's and Ricketts' divisions crossed the Upper Bridge while Doubleday's men forded the stream at Pry's Ford. Hooker's Federals leapt stone walls and pushed down fences to clear their line of march and continue their thus far unimpeded westward push. But Hooker and McClellan knew the enemy would not sit by quietly and watch.

Lee was not caught unaware by Hooker's movement though he was initially perplexed. Simultaneously, aides dashed into Lee's headquarters reporting Hooker's movement and a Federal stirring near the Lower Bridge, which turned out to be Burnside getting into position. Lee moved Hood's and J. R. Jones' divisions north of town to meet Hooker while Lawton's division marched to Lee's right. Once he discovered that the Federals did not intend to cross there, Lawton filed his men towards the army's left flank north of Sharpsburg.

By 5:00 p.m., Hooker began turning his column left so that it advanced south along the Smoketown Road. Meade's

lead brigade, led by Brig. Gen. Truman Seymour, encountered Confederate pickets and drove them back to the East Woods. There, Brig. Gen. John Hood's two deep South brigades ran into Seymour's men. The ensuing firefight grew and continued until darkness drowned it out around 6:30 p.m., leaving the two lines within close proximity to each other.

Hooker's final dispositions of the day centered around the Joseph Poffenberger farm and the North Woods. Two of his divisions faced south—the intended direction of their attack the next day—while one faced west to protect the army's right flank. Overnight, Brigadier General Joseph Mansfield's Twelfth Corps crossed

▲ Though a critic of George B. McClellan, Joseph Hooker was promoted to command of the First Corps at the beginning of the campaign. Hooker's corps was in rough shape by September 1862, but McClellan believed Hooker would "soon bring them out of the kinks & ... make them fight if anyone can." (Library of Congress)

▶ The divisions of George Meade and James Ricketts used the Upper Bridge on the afternoon of September 16 as part of George B. McClellan's opening move of the battle of Antietam. Later that night and into the next morning, Joseph Mansfield's Twelfth Corps likewise crossed here before taking up their prebattle positions. (Author's collection)

the creek at the Upper Bridge and by 2:30 a.m. on September 17, bivouacked about one mile northeast of the First Corps.

Tired from their exertions of the previous few days, Hood requested and received permission to remove his division from the army's front line. Lawton's men replaced them and loosely straddled the Smoketown Road south of the East Woods facing north and northeast. J. R. Jones' division formed on their left, west of the Hagerstown Pike.

Far from Sharpsburg, William Franklin's Sixth Corps prepared to quickly march to Sharpsburg the next morning. Couriers raced from Lee's headquarters too with orders for A. P. Hill's division to join

the army with all haste. McLaws's and Anderson's divisions marched overnight to Sharpsburg to be ready for the morning's fight.

By nightfall, quiet settled over the field on both sides of the creek except for the sporadic picket firing and soldiers' whispers. The "quiet that precedes a great battle," recalled one Northern soldier, "has something of the terrible in it." After surveying his lines for the night, Hooker told his staff officers what every soldier on the Antietam battlefield, North and South, knew: "We are through for tonight, but tomorrow we fight the battle that will decide the fate of the Republic."

# Antietam's Northern Front

From the North Woods to the Sunken Road, combat raged from 6:00 a.m. to 1:00 p.m. Nearly 58,000 soldiers from both sides were engaged; 18,000 became casualties in a space of 1.4 square miles. Names like the Cornfield, the West Woods, the Dunker Church, and the Bloody Lane became immortalized.

The first hint of daylight peaked over the crest of South Mountain around 5:00 a.m. on Wednesday, September 17, 1862. Soldiers could still gaze up at the stars when, in the East Woods, dark forms began to be discernable as men. The firefight there picked up where it left off the previous night.

Brightening daylight illuminated the Antietam battlefield and the contending battle lines. That morning, roughly 90,000 men—35,000 Confederates and 55,000 Federals—prepared to fight, with more en route.

From Nicodemus Heights in the north to Snavely's Ford in the south, Lee's line stretched nearly 3.5 miles. Much of the Confederate cavalry held the army's left with 15 guns under Major John Pelham on Nicodemus Heights. The divisions of Lawton, J. R. Jones, and Hood, under Jackson's command, held the ground from the West Woods to the Mumma farm. The command shifted to Longstreet as D. H. Hill's division extended the line from there to the Boonsboro Pike. D. R. Jones' men stretched the line south of Sharpsburg

and John Walker's division held the right of the army near Snavely's Ford. McLaws's and Anderson's recently arrived divisions grabbed a little rest west of town waiting for orders to go into the fight. A. P. Hill's division was on the way from Harpers Ferry. Lee's artillerymen manned 246 guns along the position.

Sunlight found Hooker's and Mansfield's corps on the Confederate side of the creek.

## Armament of the Armies

Opposing Union and Confederate armies throughout the Civil War fought with similar tactics, commands, and weaponry. In the Army of the Potomac, approximately 88 percent of its infantry carried rifled weapons while approximately 56 percent of the army's artillery batteries fired rifled pieces. The Army of Northern Virginia was less well-armed in terms of rifled versus smoothbore weaponry. About 67 percent of the army's infantry shouldered rifles and 47 percent of the cannons it was armed with were rifled.

# Army of Northern Virginia Order of Battle

**Army of Northern Virginia: General Robert E. Lee**

**Longstreet's Command: Maj. Gen. James Longstreet**

Jones' Division (1 battery): Brig. Gen. David R. Jones

Toombs' Brigade: Brig. Gen. Robert Toombs

Drayton's Brigade: Brig. Gen. Thomas Drayton

Garnett's Brigade: Brig. Gen. Richard Garnett

Kemper's Brigade: Brig. Gen. James Kemper

Jenkins' Brigade: Col. Joseph Walker

Anderson's Brigade: Col. George T. Anderson

Anderson's Division (4 batteries): Maj. Gen. Richard Anderson

Wilcox's Brigade: Col. Alfred Cumming

Mahone's Brigade: Col. William Parham

Featherston's Brigade: Col. Carnot Posey

Armistead's Brigade: Brig. Gen. Lewis Armistead

Pryor's Brigade: Brig. Gen. Roger Pryor

Wright's Brigade: Brig. Gen. Ambrose Wright

Hood's Division (3 batteries): Brig. Gen. John Hood

Hood's Brigade: Col. William Wofford

Law's Brigade: Col. Evander Law

Evans' Brigade (1 battery): Col. Peter Stevens

Washington Artillery (4 batteries): Col. James Walton

Lee's Artillery Battalion (6 batteries): Col. Stephen Lee

**Jackson's Command: Maj. Gen. Thomas "Stonewall" Jackson**

Ewell's Division (6 batteries): Brig. Gen. Alexander Lawton

Lawton's Brigade: Col. Marcellus Douglass

Trimble's Brigade: Col. James Walker

Hays' Brigade: Brig. Gen. Harry Hays

Early's Brigade: Brig. Gen. Jubal Early

Hill's Light Division (5 batteries): Maj. Gen. Ambrose P. Hill

Branch's Brigade: Brig. Gen. Lawrence Branch

Gregg's Brigade: Brig. Gen. Maxcy Gregg

Archer's Brigade: Brig. Gen. James Archer

Field's Brigade: Col. John Brockenbrough

Thomas' Brigade: Col. Edward Thomas

Pender's Brigade: Brig. Gen. William Pender

Jackson's Division (6 batteries): Brig. Gen. John R. Jones

Winder's Brigade: Col. Andrew Grigsby

Jones' Brigade: Capt. John Penn

Taliaferro's Brigade: Col. Edward Warren

Starke's Brigade: Brig. Gen. William Starke

**Unattached Divisions**

McLaws' Division (5 batteries): Maj. Gen. Lafayette McLaws

Kershaw's Brigade: Brig. Gen. Joseph Kershaw

Cobb's Brigade: Lt. Col. Christopher Sanders

Semmes' Brigade: Brig. Gen. Paul Semmes

Barksdale's Brigade: Brig. Gen. William Barksdale

Walker's Division (2 batteries): Brig. Gen. John Walker

Walker's Brigade: Col. Van Manning

Ransom's Brigade: Brig. Gen. Robert Ransom

Hill's Division (4 batteries): Maj. Gen. Daniel H. Hill

Ripley's Brigade: Brig. Gen. Roswell Ripley

Rodes' Brigade: Brig. Gen. Robert Rodes

Garland's Brigade: Col. Duncan McRae

Anderson's Brigade: Brig. Gen. George B. Anderson

Colquitt's Brigade: Col. Alfred Colquitt

**Reserve Artillery: Brig. Gen. William Pendleton**

Cutts' Battalion (5 batteries): Lt. Col. Allen Cutts

Jones' Battalion (4 batteries): Maj. Hilary Jones

Brown's Battalion (5 batteries): Col. J. Thompson Brown

Nelson's Battalion (5 batteries): Maj. William Nelson

Four unattached batteries

**Cavalry Division: Maj. Gen. J. E. B. Stuart**

Hampton's Brigade: Brig. Gen. Wade Hampton

Lee's Brigade: Brig. Gen. Fitzhugh Lee

Munford's Brigade: Col. Thomas Munford

Horse Artillery (3 batteries): Major John Pelham

# Army of the Potomac Order of Battle

**Army of the Potomac: Maj. Gen. George B. McClellan**

**First Corps (10 batteries): Maj. Gen. Joseph Hooker**
First Division: Brig. Gen. Abner Doubleday
    First Brigade: Col. Walter Phelps
    Second Brigade: Lt. Col. J. William Hofmann
    Third Brigade: Brig. Gen. Marsena Patrick
    Fourth Brigade: Brig. Gen. John Gibbon
Second Division: Brig. Gen. James Ricketts
    First Brigade: Brig. Gen. Abram Duryee
    Second Brigade: Col. William Christian
    Third Brigade: Brig. Gen. George Hartsuff
Third Division: Brig. Gen. George Meade
    First Brigade: Brig. Gen. Truman Seymour
    Second Brigade: Col. Albert Magilton
    Third Brigade: Lt. Col. Robert Anderson

**Second Corps (7 batteries): Maj. Gen. Edwin Sumner**
First Division: Maj. Gen. Israel Richardson
    First Brigade: Brig. Gen. John Caldwell
    Second Brigade: Brig. Gen. Thomas Meagher
    Third Brigade: Col. John Brooke
Second Division: Maj. Gen. John Sedgwick
    First Brigade: Brig. Gen. Willis Gorman
    Second Brigade: Brig. Gen. Oliver Howard
    Third Brigade: Brig. Gen. Napoleon J. T. Dana
Third Division: Brig. Gen. William French
    First Brigade: Brig. Gen. Nathan Kimball
    Second Brigade: Col. Dwight Morris
    Third Brigade: Brig. Gen. Max Weber

**Fourth Corps (attached to Sixth Corps) (4 batteries)**
First Division: Maj. Gen. Darius Couch
    First Brigade: Brig. Gen. Charles Devens Jr.
    Second Brigade: Brig. Gen. Albion Howe
    Third Brigade: Brig. Gen. John Cochrane

**Fifth Corps (15 batteries): Maj. Gen. Fitz John Porter**
First Division: Maj. Gen. George Morell
    First Brigade: Col. James Barnes
    Second Brigade: Brig. Gen. Charles Griffin
    Third Brigade: Col. Thomas Stockton
Second Division: Brig. Gen. George Sykes
    First Brigade: Lt. Col. Robert Buchanan
    Second Brigade: Maj. Charles Lovell
    Third Brigade: Col. Gouverneur Warren

Third Division: Brig. Gen. Andrew Humphreys
    First Brigade: Brig. Gen. Erastus Tyler
    Second Brigade: Col. Peter Allabach
Artillery Reserve: Lt. Col. William Hays

**Sixth Corps (7 batteries): Maj. Gen. William Franklin**
First Division: Maj. Gen. Henry Slocum
    First Brigade: Col. Alfred Torbert
    Second Brigade: Col. Joseph Bartlett
    Third Brigade: Brig. Gen. John Newton
Second Division: Maj. Gen. William F. Smith
    First Brigade: Brig. Gen. Winfield Hancock
    Second Brigade: Brig. Gen. William T. H. Brooks
    Third Brigade: Col. William Irwin

**Ninth Corps (8 batteries): Maj. Gen. Ambrose Burnside/ Brig. Gen. Jacob Cox**
First Division: Brig. Gen. Orlando Willcox
    First Brigade: Col. Benjamin Christ
    Second Brigade: Col. Thomas Welsh
Second Division: Brig. Gen. Samuel Sturgis
    First Brigade: Brig. Gen. James Nagle
    Second Brigade: Brig. Gen. Edward Ferrero
Third Division: Brig. Gen. Isaac Rodman
    First Brigade: Col. Harrison Fairchild
    Second Brigade: Col. Edward Harland
Kanawha Division: Col. Eliakim Scammon
    First Brigade: Col. Hugh Ewing
    Second Brigade: Col. George Crook

**Twelfth Corps (7 batteries): Brig. Gen. Joseph Mansfield**
First Division: Brig. Gen. Alpheus Williams
    First Brigade: Brig. Gen. Samuel Crawford
    Third Brigade: Brig. Gen. George Gordon
Second Division: Brig. Gen. George Greene
    First Brigade: Lt. Col. Hector Tyndale
    Second Brigade: Col. Henry Stainrook
    Third Brigade: Col. William Goodrich

**Cavalry Division (6 batteries): Brig. Gen. Alfred Pleasonton**
    First Brigade: Maj. Charles Whiting
    Second Brigade: Col. John Farnsworth
    Third Brigade: Col. Richard Rush
    Fourth Brigade: Col. Andrew McReynolds
    Fifth Brigade: Col. Benjamin Davis

# Dunker Church

The white-washed walls of the Dunker Church were erected by the German Baptist Brethren along the Hagerstown Pike in 1852. Known as Dunkers because of their use of full-immersion baptism, members of this religious sect dressed and lived modestly. They were pacifists who did not condone military service, stressed human brotherhood and were thus opposed to slavery, and practiced temperance. Sharpsburg's Dunker Church survived the battle despite being heavily damaged. The Dunkers renovated it and continued to worship there until the end of the 19th century. In 1921, a windstorm toppled the structure. In 1962, it was reconstructed using some of the original materials.

On the east side of the creek running from north to south was Sumner's Second Corps, Porter's Fifth Corps, and Burnside's Ninth Corps. Franklin's men left Pleasant Valley that morning headed for Sharpsburg. Hunt commanded 293 artillery pieces.

Joseph Hooker did not like being isolated west of the creek. As the brightening daylight revealed the high ground one mile south of the North Woods (the Dunker Church plateau) and the nearby whitewashed walls of the Dunker Church, Hooker ordered his men to make that pacifist church their objective. "I desired to take the initiative," Hooker later testified, to punch before he was punched.

He resolved to advance on a two-division front. Abner Doubleday's division advanced south along the Hagerstown Pike while James Ricketts' men moved along the Smoketown Road. Hooker kept Meade's division in reserve.

Artillery began the fight. Pelham's guns on Nicodemus Heights opened fire, followed by Stephen Lee's 19 guns on the Dunker Church plateau.

As the rising sun revealed more of the deployments, Seymour's brigade cleared the East Woods and resumed their fight, engaging the right of Colonel Marcellus Douglass' brigade as well as Colonel James Walker's North Carolinians and Georgians. The heavy Federal batteries across the creek added their metal to the fight and the Confederates got the worst of the Yankee

▶ Joseph Hooker set his sights on the high ground across the Hagerstown Pike from the Dunker Church as his objective. (Author's collection)

bullets and shells. Ammunition ran out for the Federals after 45 minutes of shooting, but help was on the way for Seymour's men.

Ricketts' division moved to Seymour's support. Brig. Gen. George Hartsuff's brigade held Ricketts' right and Colonel William Christian's brigade formed on his left. Bad luck plagued the two brigades from the start. Hartsuff went down with a wound that paralyzed his brigade for 30 minutes. Christian mentally snapped under the artillery barrage and fled the field.

Brigadier General Abram Duryee's brigade moved into the void. They sidestepped Hartsuff's frozen line and pushed into a 24-acre cornfield grown by David R. Miller and his family, whose home stood near the field's northwest corner. At 6:00 a.m., Duryee's men reached the cornfield's southern edge. Douglass' men firing down their "own corn row" greeted the Federal troops. Duryee's left pushed beyond the corn briefly before the fire of Douglass' and Walker's infantry and Stephen Lee's 19 guns on the Dunker Church Plateau forced them back. The brigade battled alone for thirty minutes and suffered 33 percent losses. Douglass' skirmishers pursued them into the corn.

▲ Major John Pelham was a rising star in the Army of Northern Virginia in 1862. Known for his good looks, Pelham excelled in the art of horse artillery. (Library of Congress)

◀ Col. Marcellus Douglass's Georgia brigade were the first Confederates to receive Union attackers after they moved through Miller's cornfield on the morning of September 17. This image of the cornfield was taken from Douglass's position. (Author's collection)

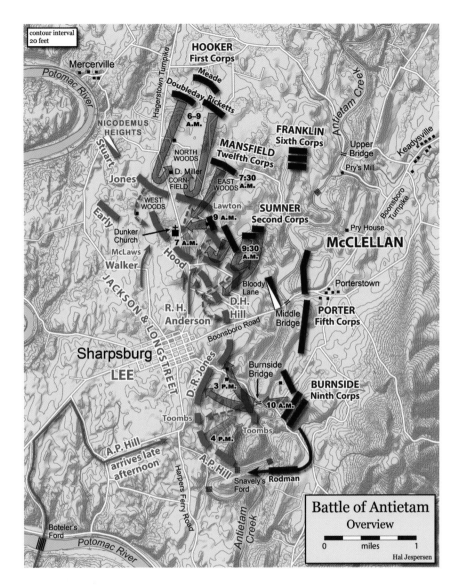

**Battle of Antietam**

Overview

0       miles       1

Hal Jespersen

Hartsuff's brigade, now led by Colonel Richard Coulter, restarted its forward movement at 6:40 a.m. Colonel Peter Lyle, now commanding Christian's brigade, supported Hartsuff's left. Harry Hays' Louisiana brigade reinforced Douglass' right and attacked towards the cornfield. The two sides suffered severely. The 12th Massachusetts, one of Coulter's regiments, carried 334 men into the fight and lost 224 casualties. Hays' Louisianans lost 323 of 550 men while Walker's brigade, approximately 700 strong, lost its commander to a serious wound along with 237 men.

Along the Hagerstown Pike, Doubleday's fight began at 6:30 a.m. These men had suffered under enemy artillery fire since before dawn in their positions on the Poffenberger farm. John Gibbon's brigade spearheaded Doubleday's attack. Col. Walter Phelps' and Brig. Gen. Marsena Patrick's brigades supported the Midwesterners.

Gibbon's brigade advanced through the Miller farm in two lines. Confederate skirmishers in the front line of Jones' division west of the pike peppered the front line. Gibbon sent his two rear regiments across the road to clear this threat; Doubleday dispatched Patrick's New Yorkers with them.

The Wisconsin regiments in the front reached the south fence line bordering the cornfield and immediately received a wall of lead from the thinning ranks of Douglass' stout Georgia troops. Gibbon's Yankees leaped over the fence into the open field south of the cornfield. Supported by Phelps' men, Gibbon's withering fire meant forced Douglass' line back. Division commander Lawton was wounded, Marcellus Douglass died after being hit for the eighth time, and the brigade limped to the rear with a 49 percent casualty rate.

Doubleday's men west of the pike encountered J. R. Jones' division arrayed in two lines. Jones was stunned by a shell early and passed command to Brigadier General William Starke as he left the field. Colonel Andrew Grigsby led the 450 men of two brigades in Jones' front line. Faced with flanking fire from the Union regiments in the West Woods, they did not hold for long. Gibbon's advance along the pike and through the northern edge of the West Woods beyond Grigsby's left forced them back upon the second line.

Starke led the second line—two brigades totaling 1,150 men—to Grigsby's support. These supporting Southerners jumped up and aimed their charge for the right of Gibbon's and Phelps' men who had just cleared Douglass' line from the field. Some confusion hampered the advance and Starke fell mortally wounded leading it. Nonetheless, his men made it to the stout rail fences lining the Hagerstown Pike. They found the enemy within easy range on the opposite side of the road. The two sides shredded each other with volleys at point blank range for fifteen minutes.

▼ Photographs of the dead of the Antietam battlefield shocked the American public. The photos were, in many ways, the birth of photojournalism. These dead Confederates lay along the fences bordering the Hagerstown Pike. (Library of Congress)

▲ John Bell Hood proved many times his worth to the Army of Northern Virginia. An able and aggressive commander, Hood's assault blunted Hooker's thrust but at a terrible cost—nearly half his division, 1,025 men, were casualties. (Library of Congress)

best fighting men in Robert E. Lee's army. Lawton's men replaced them the night of September 16 so Hood's men could eat and rest. In the midst of preparing their meals, the call from Lawton and Jackson for support arrived and deprived the men of their long-sought-after meal.

As Hood's men crossed the Hagerstown Pike and spilled into the open field east of it, they came under fire from a number of Federal batteries clustering on the hill north of the cornfield. In all, as many as 18 guns punched holes in Hood's advancing formation.

Hood's attack first splintered into two parts, and then broke apart several more times as the advance continued. Colonel William Wofford's brigade, the famed Texas Brigade, on the left of the division line aimed for the southwest corner of the cornfield. There, they would be in position to fend off the Federals firing into Hood's left. Colonel Evander Law led his brigade towards the detached 90th Pennsylvania at the southeastern corner of the cornfield.

The Pennsylvanians stood alone in Law's front and quickly melted away for the rear with a nearly 50 percent casualty rate. Law's rightmost regiment, the 4th Alabama, continued into the East Woods, where the 5th Texas from Wofford's brigade and a battalion of Georgians from Colquitt's brigade joined them.

Law's remaining regiments pushed into the cornfield. At its northern boundary, George Meade's two Pennsylvania Reserve brigades shook into battle lines and awaited the Confederate onslaught. Lieutenant Colonel Robert Anderson's brigade held Meade's right near the Hagerstown Pike. Col. Albert Magilton's four regiments extended the line to the East Woods. Hood's men fired on them as they formed.

Law's brigade, whittled down to North Carolinians and Mississippians following

In the enthusiasm of their advance and their attention focused on the enemy's battle line in their front, Starke's men failed to see the remainder of Gibbon's and Patrick's men slip behind their left and find a rock ledge in their rear. Also, a battery of Federal artillery led by Captain Joseph Campbell deployed on their left flank and opened fire. The Confederates could not hold under a three-sided fire and withdrew back to the West Woods, leaving 470 of their men behind on the field. Hooker's surge continued south towards the Dunker Church.

When Hooker's men came within about 400 yards of the plateau, a new enemy line emerged from the West Woods. John Bell Hood's ranks were filled with 2,000 of the

the detachment of the Alabama troops, pressed into the cornfield into the face of canister fired from the Federal guns on the elevation to their north. Battlefield confusion soon aided Law's men. Once Magilton's brigade reached the cornfield's north boundary, Hooker ordered Meade to dispatch a brigade into the East Woods to shore up the corps' left flank. Magilton's men turned to their left and began executing the order when Law's men stormed into their ranks.

Magilton's two center regiments broke under the pressure of Law's fire. The 8th Pennsylvania Reserves on the left stoutly fired from the cover of the East Woods while the 7th Pennsylvania Reserves on the right lent their lead to the effort. Two Federal batteries behind Magilton's crumbling line gave up the fight, leaving Captain Dunbar Ransom's Regular artillery battery to deal with the worsening situation. Some of Law's men of the 2nd and 11th Mississippi crossed the fence. They did not advance far, however, before the natural friction weighing on any Civil War attack and the arrival of Mansfield's lead elements convinced the Southerners to abandon their breakthrough.

To the west, Wofford's men pressed on. Fearful of an attack from on his left flank from a body of Union troops along the Hagerstown Pike, Hood ordered three of Wofford's regiments to oblique in that direction and face west to confront the enemy. Along the stout fence lining the road, they met Federal infantry fire and blasts of canister from Campbell's Regular battery. Wofford's infantrymen still neared the guns though, and killed or wounded over a dozen of the gunners. Gibbon brought more infantry west of the pike to support them.

The 1st Texas, still advancing north, was supposed to halt at the south edge of

the cornfield and align with the rest of the brigade. Their blood was up after driving the enemy and having their breakfast disturbed by the call to battle. Either failing to receive the order to halt or paying no attention to it, they plunged into the corn. Meade's Pennsylvanians waited for the Texans to come within 30 yards before they squeezed their triggers and ripped apart the Texans' ranks. The 1st Texas ran from the fire which dropped 82 percent of its men.

▲ George Meade's Pennsylvania Reserves stopped John Bell Hood's counterattack into Hooker's lines. Meade later praised his men, particularly Capt. Dunbar Ransom's artillery battery, for "repulsing the enemy" during "one of the critical periods of the morning." (Library of Congress)

With Law's brigade and the 1st Texas withdrawing, Hood's left had to do the same. Hood's brigades departed the field roughly handled. Wofford's brigade lost 65 percent of its strength. To their right, Law's men suffered about 40 percent casualties.

Campbell's battery that tore gaps in Wofford's line lost 40 men, 26 horses killed, and 7 horses disabled, the highest loss of any battery at Antietam. Its 15-year-old bugler, Johnny Cook, stepped in to man the guns, winning the Medal of Honor. Gibbon ordered the devastated battery back from the firing line.

Federals now pursued Hood's division from two directions. Anderson's brigade pushed through the cornfield. As they did, one Pennsylvanian picked up the Lone Star flag of the 1st Texas. He had to pry it from underneath "thirteen dead men lying on and around it." One of Anderson's regiments pushed south of the corn. From

the west, elements of Gibbon's and Patrick's brigades advanced towards the knoll near the southwest corner of the cornfield. After crowning the knoll, the low ground in front of them revealed Brig. Gen. Roswell Ripley's brigade arriving from the burning Mumma farm—Ripley's men had set it on fire—to shore up the Confederate left.

Both sides sent more men to the growing fight around the cornfield. Mansfield's 7,500-man Twelfth Corps moved to Hooker's support at daybreak and reached the field as Hood's attack peaked. D. H. Hill's division also began sliding to the Confederate left.

In the bigger picture, McClellan decided to send more troops to support Hooker and follow up on the success McClellan believed Hooker had achieved—this moments before Hood's troops knocked the First Corps out of the fight. Two divisions of Maj. Gen. Edwin Sumner's Second Corps—

▼ The Mumma family lost everything when their home and barn burned early on September 17. The flames consumed almost all of their earthly possessions, as well. Samuel Mumma Jr., the eldest Mumma son, wrote after the war that the damages to their property totaled "from $8,000 to $10,000." Though civilians were often compensated for damages done to their property, the Mummas did not even receive a cent. However, they managed to rebuild their home by the next summer. (Library of Congress)

Sedgwick's and French's—received orders to move across the creek. The corps' third division, Richardson's, was not released until Maj. Gen. George Morell's Fifth Corps division relieved it. McClellan gave Sumner his orders at 7:20 a.m. The Second Corps marched towards the East Woods listening to the sounds of battle.

The Union push that cleared Hood's division from the cornfield ran into the lead elements of D. H. Hill's division after passing into the field south of Miller's cornfield. Brig. Gen. Roswell Ripley left the fight early with a wound, turning over command to Colonel George Doles. This mixed-state brigade crossed the Smoketown Road and drove Anderson's, Gibbon's, and Patrick's men back. Part of the brigade faced west to protect their flank while the right regiments surged towards the cornfield.

Immediately after driving the First Corps remnants back, Ripley's men encountered Mansfield's deploying corps. Brig. Gen. Alpheus Williams' division moved into position north of the cornfield between the Hagerstown Pike and the East Woods. To their left, Brigadier General George Greene's division formed.

Mansfield's corps underwent a near instant command change when it arrived on the firing line. Confusing enemy troops in front of one of his regiments for Hooker's withdrawing men, Mansfield rode in front of the 10th Maine, ordering them to cease fire. A Mainer pointed out the general's error. Before Mansfield could return to safety, a bullet hit him in the chest and forced him from the field. He died the next day. Alpheus Williams assumed command of the corps.

Brigadier General Samuel Crawford's brigade was a mix of veterans and rookies. One of the rookie regiments, the 128th Pennsylvania, in quick succession lost

▲ Joseph Mansfield took command of the Twelfth Corps on September 15, 1862. More than half the troops he commanded lacked any battlefield experience. Both their and their commander's novelty to battlefield situations showed. (Library of Congress)

its colonel and lieutenant colonel. The regiment's major ordered the disorganized line to charge into the cornfield. Doles' fire stopped it at the south fence.

Simultaneously, Brigadier General George Gordon's Federal brigade was deploying around the Miller farm. Gordon's men opened fire and caused considerable havoc in Doles' ranks. Alfred Colquitt's brigade, fresh off their successful stand at Turner's Gap, arrived to support their comrades. These new troops moved

## Profile: Major General Edwin Sumner, 1797–1863

Edwin Sumner was the oldest general at the battle of Antietam. He was born in the 18th century—January 30, 1797—in Boston. He did not attend West Point. Instead, he received a commission into the United States Army in 1819. His army career was mostly populated fighting Indians out west, though he was an active participant in the Mexican-American War. There, he received two brevet

▼ Edwin Sumner.
(Library of Congress)

promotions followed by a full promotion at the conclusion of the conflict. Back in the west afterward, Sumner became involved in "Bleeding Kansas," where he dealt with personalities such as John Brown, a freedom fighter looking to make Kansas a territory free of slavery. At the Civil War's outset, Sumner was one of three Regular Army brigadier generals. During George B. McClellan's organization of the Army of the Potomac in 1861–62, Sumner received command of the army's Second Corps. He fought his corps well during the Peninsula Campaign and Seven Days Campaign, publicly earning McClellan's praise, but privately the army commander was skeptical of Sumner's abilities as a battlefield general. He was always aggressive on the battlefield and personally led his men into battle. Sumner commanded the center column of the Army of the Potomac during its advance into Maryland in September 1862. Once his corps crossed Antietam Creek on September 17, 1862, and fought in the West Woods and at the Sunken Road, Sumner became the senior commander on that end of the battlefield. He led Ambrose Burnside's Left Grand Division at the battle of Fredericksburg. Sumner resigned from the army when Joseph Hooker ascended to lead the Army of the Potomac. He received new orders to take command of the Department of the Missouri, but he never did. He died on his way to his new post on March 21, 1863.

into the cornfield. Gordon's brigade and Ransom's gunners stopped the advance.

Then, another of Hill's brigades arrived. Garland's brigade, led by Colonel Duncan McRae, extended Colquitt's right, which inspired Colquitt's men to renew their attack. Some of the regiments reached the cornfield's northern boundary. McRae's support for Colquitt did not last long. Already in a state of confusion, the North Carolina brigade panicked at the sight of a Union battle line beyond their right and fled. Hill watched this from the rear and realized the futility of the actions of his three brigades. He ordered them to withdraw.

Before Hill could extricate his men, Greene's division hit them hard. Colonel William Goodrich's brigade supported the Federal line along the Hagerstown Pike. The division's other two brigades, Lieutenant Colonel Hector Tyndale's and Colonel Henry Stainrook's, deployed into the East Woods. Tyndale's right caught Colquitt's 6th Georgia in the northeast corner of the cornfield and nearly destroyed the unit in a hand-to-hand fight. Low estimates of the 6th Georgia's losses begin at 75 percent, and the actual figure may have been higher. Stainrook's line cleared the hodgepodge of Georgians, Alabamans, and Texans out of the East Woods. By 9:00 a.m., Greene's men occupied the Dunker Church Plateau. The

▲ "Cease firing, they are our own men!" Mansfield yelled to soldiers of the 10th Maine Infantry shortly before falling mortally wounded. He died the next morning. This mortuary cannon marks the approximate location of Mansfield's mortal wounding. Five similar markers denote the locations of Antietam's five other generals killed or mortally wounded on September 17. (Author's collection)

▶ Alpheus Williams proved to be a reliable commander throughout the war, though his lack of a West Point degree may have held him back from deserved promotions. He handled the Twelfth Corps ably after Mansfield's mortal wounding. (Library of Congress)

125th Pennsylvania advanced into the West Woods behind the Dunker Church.

In three hours of intense fighting, both sides suffered a combined 8,000 casualties in the fight centering on Miller's cornfield. Starke's and Lawton's divisions were nearly fought out, having suffered 33 percent and 50 percent casualties, respectively. Hood's losses exceeded 50 percent. Hooker's First Corps was hardly better off. The corps lost 27 percent of its strength, though one division commander admitted he could not gather more than 300 men from the entire corps. Hooker himself was wounded in the foot and had to leave the field. Fighting whittled the Twelfth Corps down to about 6,000 men.

Edwin Sumner rode into the East Woods around 9:00 a.m. and quickly deduced his corps would have to take over the fight. He determined the West Woods was the key to the northern end of the battlefield and, with no Confederates visible before him,

ordered Major General John Sedgwick's 5,500-man division to secure the woods and roll up Lee's left. Brigadier General William French's division was supposed to support Sedgwick's left. However, French mistook Greene's division, who were without ammunition, for Sedgwick and turned his own division south. Mistaking Greene's stationary division, awaiting more ammunition in a swale in front of the Dunker Church, for Sedgwick, French led his men south away from Sedgwick.

Sedgwick's division advanced across the bloodied landscape between the East and West woods in three brigade lines, led from front to back by brigadier generals Willis Gorman, Napoleon Dana, and Oliver Howard. At 9:15 a.m., Gorman's men crossed the Hagerstown Pike and entered the West Woods. At the woods' western end, a scrabbled line of Confederate infantry and 24 guns overseen by J. E. B. Stuart stopped Gorman's—and Sedgwick's—advance. The remaining brigades, unable to engage the enemy in front, stacked up behind Gorman.

Sedgwick's line in the woods was not seamless, though. During the advance, Gorman's left regiment, the 34th New York, drifted away from the rest of the brigade, opening a 300-yard gap.

Besides Stuart's line deployed on Houser's Ridge, Brigadier General Jubal Early's 1,100 Virginians were active. Early's men, who had spent the morning protecting Pelham's artillery on Nicodemus Heights, now moved south, deflecting a limited Federal advance in the northern West Woods before passing south to confront the 125th Pennsylvania. When he arrived there, Early saw help arriving.

Just as the cornfield fight drew additional Federal strength to the battlefield's northern end, now at mid-morning it was the weight of Lee's army leaning in that direction. Hill's withdrawal prompted a call to army headquarters for more troops. A similar request came from Jackson. Having already sent Colonel George T. Anderson's brigade from Cemetery Hill to his left, Lee also called for McLaws's division to break its bivouac west of town and support the army's left. Lee personally began to scrape together a line of artillery on Reel Ridge west of the Hagerstown Pike. Then, he called Walker's division from his right at Snavely's Ford to march to the opposite end of the battlefield.

▲ John Sedgwick's division suffered an astounding 2,228 casualties in the West Woods—40 percent of the division's strength— in less than 30 minutes of fighting. Sedgwick himself was wounded; later, he became the highest-ranking Federal general killed during the Civil War. (Library of Congress)

▶ Numerically, no regiment, Union or Confederate, suffered worse casualties than the 15th Massachusetts Infantry. By the end of the day, the regiment lost 318 men killed or wounded of the 606 it took into action—a 52 percent casualty rate. (Author's collection)

By 9 a.m., approximately 90 percent of Lee's infantry was north of or heading north of Sharpsburg. While these troops would buttress the defense of the army's left, Lee had not given up the hope that, if an opportunity presented itself, they could crush the Federal right and achieve the battlefield victory north of the Potomac River that he had come into Maryland seeking.

Sedgwick's stalled division turned out to be an inviting target. It was not design, but chance, that brought McLaws's division hurtling toward Sedgwick's exposed left. Four thousand men in five Confederate brigades aligned from left to right: Brig. Gen. Paul Semmes, Early, Brig. Gen. William Barksdale, Anderson, and Brig. Gen. Joseph Kershaw.

At Jackson's request, Semmes' brigade went to support Stuart's line. They advanced across an open field under heavy fire of the 606-man 15th Massachusetts. The two lines engaged at approximately 150 yards. Some of the men in Dana's brigade tried to fire through the 15th Massachusetts. Overall,

the New England regiment lost 330 men in the fight.

Near the Dunker Church, Barksdale's brigade arrived to support Early's men in their fight against the 125th Pennsylvania. The 34th New York and 7th Michigan came to help the rookie Pennsylvanians but the combined pressure of Early, Barksdale, and parts of Kershaw's and Anderson's brigades cracked the Federal left and the Confederates worked their way into the gap in Sedgwick's lines.

Confederates slammed north into Sedgwick's flank. Federal commanders tried to face their men south to stop the onslaught but the enemy's momentum carried them forward and Sedgwick's division unraveled. "My God, we must get out of this," Sumner exclaimed when he learned what was transpiring. Howard's brigade crumbled first followed by the other two. Some regiments paused briefly to resist as they fell back north. Quickly assembled Union stopgaps, including a westward forlorn charge by two Twelfth Corps regiments, a buildup of Federal

▼ The terrain of the Sunken Road has not changed much since 1862. The United States War Department constructed the observation tower in 1897 to provide a unique view to battlefield visitors. (Author's collection)

artillery, and the natural friction of offensive maneuvers stopped the Confederate attack short of the North Woods.

In twenty minutes, Sedgwick's division suffered the highest casualty rate of any Union division on the Antietam battlefield. Out of 5,500 men that entered the West Woods, Sedgwick lost 40 percent of his men in less than thirty minutes. Sedgwick himself was wounded three times.

The West Woods action was the only point on September 17 where more Confederates were engaged than Federals. Lee's army was still a dangerous foe that demonstrated its offensive potential.

The Confederate surge also carried some of the brigades east across the Hagerstown Pike. Three regiments of Kershaw's brigade charged up the western slope of the Dunker Church Plateau only to be repulsed by Greene's resupplied division. Colonel Van Manning of Walker's division also sent three regiments across the pike to recapture the key terrain feature and met a similar fate. Victoriously, Greene's men, totaling 1,350 soldiers, pushed into the West Woods beyond the Dunker Church and assumed a position that faced both south and west.

While opposing forces slugged it out among the trees of the West Woods, French's division ran into two of D. H. Hill's brigades in a sunken farm lane that meandered from the Hagerstown Pike north of Sharpsburg to the Boonsboro Pike east of town. The main part of Hill's line stretched about 600 yards and consisted of Robert Rodes' Alabamans and George B. Anderson's North Carolinians. Remnants of Hill's division beaten earlier in the day and Cobb's brigade held the left of the line.

Hill's men used the roadbed for movement earlier in the day. The high ground above the road concealed the columns from the watchful eyes of Federal

▼ William French's division consisted of more untested soldiers than veterans as it attacked the Sunken Road. In fact, the division had only been formed the day before the battle. (Library of Congress)

artillerymen. At 9:30 a.m., the front line of French's division attacked and pinned them in the road.

French's division, 5,700 strong, consisted of ten regiments. Seven of them went into combat for the first time on September 17, 1862. Like Sedgwick's, the division marched into battle with its three brigades stacked up one behind the other. Brigadier General Max Weber's brigade was in front. Colonel Dwight Morris' brigade trailed it while Brigadier General Nathan Kimball's line brought up the rear. The rookie troops fully comprised Weber's and Morris' brigades.

When Weber's line reached the crest of the ridge running on both sides of the Roulette farm lane, Confederate musket fire warmly greeted it. In five minutes, 450 of Weber's 1,800 men were casualties. The triumphant Confederates charged out of the road to drive the Federals from the high ground but were quickly pushed back. Morris' brigade fared similarly.

This action occurred concurrently with Sedgwick's fight and withdrawal. Sumner ordered French "to push on and make a diversion in favor of Sedgwick." French called Kimball's brigade to the front line. Despite the experience of Kimball and three of his four regiments, they could not advance and break Hill's line; they could only keep up a hot fire against it. Having suffered 1,750 casualties within an hour, French's division was neutralized.

After having personally visited the Sunken Road line before the fight began, Lee recognized the weakness and importance of the position one mile from Sharpsburg. He ordered his last reserve, Maj. Gen. Richard Anderson's division, to move to Hill's support. They crossed the Hagerstown Pike onto the Piper farm about 10:30. Anderson's artillery deployed first but failed to silence Captain John Tompkins' Rhode Island battery to their

north, meaning the infantry had to go in under their fire and that of the guns of position across Antietam Creek as it looked to extend Hill's right. From there, it would be in position to hit French's exposed left.

Anderson's division encountered immediate problems. The capable Anderson went down early with a thigh wound. Command passed to the politician turned general Roger Pryor. Under Pryor's command (he may not have known it was his), the division advanced piecemeal to the road.

Brigadier General Ambrose Wright's brigade went first. They advanced through the Piper orchard and cornfield to beyond G. B. Anderson's right. The brigade tried to solicit help from the North Carolinians to charge Kimball's line. Only the 3rd Georgia on the brigade's right made a real effort. Kimball's leftmost regiment, the 7th West Virginia, turned to face the threat. Their fire, combined with that of the guns of position, drove another halfhearted Confederate attack back to the lane. Pryor's other brigades—his own, Colonel Carnot Posey's, and Colonel Alfred Cumming's— jumped into the lane to support George B. Anderson's right center.

The loss of Confederate officers in the road spread confusion and chaos among the Confederate ranks. Brig. Gen. George B. Anderson was wounded and carried from the field (he later died from it). Two of Richard Anderson's brigade commanders also went down with wounds, as did numerous regimental and company commanders in both divisions.

Arriving Federals of Major General Israel B. Richardson's Second Corps division soon tipped the battle in the bluecoats' favor. Richardson's 4,000 soldiers crossed the creek about 9:30 a.m. once Morell's division relieved them. They arrived behind French's battle line minutes after Anderson's division first pitched into the fight.

Brigadier General Thomas Meagher's Irish Brigade advanced south of the Roulette farm lane. Pushing through French's line, Meagher ordered his men to fix bayonets as French's brigades had done. The native Irishman believe one or two volleys followed by a bayonet charge would break the Confederate line. The same fire that ground up French's three lines dispelled Meagher's men of any notion of a quick conclusion to their day. They settled in atop the ridge and slugged it out with the enemy in their front. "It was give and take until ammunition ran out," said a brigade officer.

Being on the firing line for some time thinned Meagher's ranks. The two lines were close enough that insults hurtled between the battle lines above the din of battle. The 29th Massachusetts' commander, Lieutenant Colonel Joseph Barnes, saw from the relatively protected position they occupied the state of the brigade and feared this war of words might induce a Confederate attack. Barnes ordered his own advance before the enemy organized theirs.

From the Confederate perspective in the road, Barnes' solo advance appeared to be too much to handle. Confederates intermingled from multiple commands could not sort themselves out as officers fell by the score. Wright's and Cumming's brigades had already left the road. Now, it was the turn of Posey's and Pryor's brigades and the two right regiments of Anderson's brigade.

At the same time, Rodes' line was fracturing. The 6th Alabama occupied the hinge in Hill's line and was receiving fire from two directions. Its original commander, Col. John Gordon, was down with five wounds, ceding command to 23-year-old Lieutenant Colonel James Lightfoot. He requested and received permission from Rodes to pull the right end

▲ Just 27 years old at Antietam, Col. Francis Barlow led the combined 61st/64th New York Infantry regiments in the fighting at the Sunken Road and Piper farm. Barlow received two wounds during the battle. (Library of Congress)

of his line back. To execute the movement, Lightfoot ordered his men to turn their backs to the enemy. Panic quickly ensued, and Rodes' brigade peeled out of the road.

This left only the 2nd and 14th North Carolina to hold the Sunken Road. Brigadier General John Caldwell's brigade relieved the Irish Brigade just as the Confederate line broke. The two North Carolina regiments staggered Caldwell's right, the 61st/64th New York led by Colonel Francis Barlow. The intrepid colonel withdrew under cover, moved his men beyond the right flank of the Confederates still in the road, advanced his men again and poured a devastating enfilade fire upon them. Those were still alive surrendered. Before noon, the Sunken Road position fell to the Federals.

Richardson, the ranking Union commander on this part of the battlefield, ordered his men beyond the road towards the Piper farm and, beyond it, Sharpsburg. Immediately, they faced Confederate efforts to stymie it.

James Longstreet began these efforts before the Sunken Road fell. Aware of the increasing pressure on the right end of Hill's and Anderson's lines, Longstreet ordered two regiments under Colonel John Cooke and Cobb's brigade from McLaws's division deployed west of the Hagerstown Pike to attack Kimball's right. Moving down from Reel Ridge, Cooke's men struck Greene's left in the West Woods at the same time as soldiers under Brigadier General

Robert Ransom attacked Greene's right. The pressure forced him out of the woods.

Cooke's men pushed across the Dunker Church Plateau into the Mumma cornfield. Federal troops oriented their lines to face Cooke and the arriving Sixth Corps fired into Cooke's left flank. Cooke withdrew. Without support, Cobb's brigade followed suit.

Hill and Longstreet took extreme countermeasures to halt the Union breakthrough. Longstreet ordered his staff officers to man an abandoned cannon while he held their horses' reins. Hill personally orchestrated small counterattacks against both ends of the breakthrough. Despite the

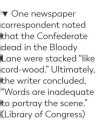

▼ One newspaper correspondent noted that the Confederate dead in the Bloody Lane were stacked "like cord-wood." Ultimately, the writer concluded, "Words are inadequate to portray the scene." (Library of Congress)

long odds, Lee's decision to cover Reel Ridge with artillery paid off. Richardson only had six smoothbore guns at his disposal and Reel Ridge was out of range of the guns of position. Twenty-five Confederate guns deployed on Reel Ridge and the Piper farm. Though three New York regiments reached the Piper Lane, they could not stay there.

Richardson's and French's men were scattered and outgunned. Richardson ordered the Second Corps soldiers back to the north side of the Sunken Road and told the battery with him to stop firing and conserve ammunition "in order that it might advance with his division at a signal then expected from Major-General Sumner." That order never materialized. A Confederate shell wounded Richardson and he had to be carried from the field. He died on November 3, 1862. The fight for the newly christened Bloody Lane was over by 1 p.m.

By that time on the northern end of the field, three Union corps had attacked the Confederate left. Each of them met with limited success but failed to deliver the knockout blow where McClellan intended it to land. The task to stabilize the Federal right fell to Sumner.

Sumner's response to Sedgwick's defeat in the West Woods was to shore up the Federal right against a dangerous enemy, namely with artillery. By noon, this gun line, a grand battery, stretched one mile in length from the Smoketown Road to Poffenberger Hill north of the North Woods. Sixty-eight guns from four corps covered the open space between the East and West Woods, precluding any serious Confederate offensives on the northern end of the field. Sumner pieced together the infantry of the First and Twelfth corps and Sedgwick's division to support the gun line.

McClellan was also aware of the shaky condition of his right and the importance of not letting it falter. Fortunately, Franklin's

▲ Israel Richardson was the first Union general to arrive on the Antietam battlefield on September 15 and the last to leave it. He died in the Pry House from his Antietam wounds. (Library of Congress)

Sixth Corps arrived behind the Union lines east of the creek about 10:00 a.m. after a ten-mile march. Having originally slotted them into the army's reserve, Lee's "opposition on the right ... rendered necessary at once to send this corps to the assistance of the right wing," explained McClellan.

Once it reached the west side of the creek, Sumner began deploying Franklin's corps as support to the Union right. Colonel William Irwin's brigade pushed towards the West Woods after repulsing Cooke's attack but was stopped short of the woods and sought cover on the Dunker Church Plateau.

When Franklin arrived on the field with the remainder of the corps, he planned to attack into the woods near the church. Sumner, however, with the fate of Sedgwick's division fresh in his mind, called off the attack. If Franklin's attack failed, "the right would be entirely routed," Sumner reasoned. Franklin pulled one of McClellan's nearby staffers and requested the commanding general's opinion.

Not for the first time that day, McClellan crossed to the west side of the creek. McClellan rode with the optimism that an attack would be made. Seeing the condition of his right for himself made McClellan feel "the aspect of affairs was anything but promising." McClellan sided with Sumner and no further attacks were made.

Robert E. Lee also looked north and contemplated an attack. Lee tasked Jackson with formulating an offensive against the Federal right. Jackson turned to Stuart to undertake a turning movement of the Federal right. Once Stuart was successful and the sound of his guns reached Jackson's ears, McLaws's and Walker's brigades would receive orders to attack out of the West Woods across the Hagerstown Pike. Stuart's attempt at about 3:30 p.m. failed to produce results. The Federal grand battery did its job and persuaded Jackson and Stuart that no attack against it across open ground would succeed.

Both commanders' failures to take the offensive and wrest the initiative firmly into their grasp did not end the fight north of Sharpsburg. The last sputter of combat swirled across the Piper farm at 5 p.m. when the 181 men of the 7th Maine received orders from Irwin to clear enemy skirmishers from the farm. The regiment's colonel recognized the futility of the matter and quickly ordered a retreat through the Piper orchard. They lost 88 men in the attack.

The 1.4 square miles from the East Woods to Houser's Ridge, from the bend of the Bloody Lane to the North Woods witnessed some of the most intense combat of the Civil War. In all, 31,000 engaged Federals lost 9,400 men, or 30 percent of its combatants north of Sharpsburg. The Army of Northern Virginia fielded 27,000 men and suffered 8,500 casualties, or 31 percent of their strength.

The intensity of the fighting and its back-and-forth nature here shaped the battle of Antietam. It was here where both commanders distributed most of their forces and where Antietam's outcome was decided. The Army of the Potomac took little ground from the Army of Northern Virginia, but its determination to hold what ground it had taken boxed Lee in between the bends of the Potomac River with his back to Virginia.

▶ "In the time I am writing every stalk of corn in the northern and greater part of the field was cut as closely as could have been done with a knife, and the slain lay in rows precisely as they had stood in their ranks a few moments before," wrote Joseph Hooker. In the area around the cornfield, there were nearly 14,000 casualties between the two sides by the end of September 17. (Author's collection)

# Antietam's Southern Front

Antietam's southern front straddled the Boonsboro Pike and involved the fight for Lee's center and right by the Fifth and Ninth corps. This sector of the battlefield included fighting near the Middle Bridge, Lower (Burnside) Bridge, and the Final Attack on the edges of Sharpsburg. About 18,000 men engaged on this part of the field; some 3,500 became casualties.

Generals Ambrose Burnside and Jacob Cox stood atop a knoll east of the Lower Bridge that bloody morning. Their Ninth Corps troops were ready, yet so far, they had been resigned to the role of spectator of the fight unfolding north of Sharpsburg. Their vantage point allowed them to see little of the actual fighting, but they could monitor the battle's progress by tracking the cloud of battle smoke and listening to the thunder of cannon and musketry.

Before 10:00 a.m., a horseman from army headquarters rode up to the pair, saluted, and presented the two men with a note. Timestamped 9:10 a.m., it read in part, "General McClellan desires you to open your attack." Burnside handed the note to Cox, and the Ninth Corps' fight began.

The Maryland Campaign was the corps' first fight with the Army of the Potomac. McClellan nonetheless entrusted the toughest task any Union corps had to face to his old friend Burnside. In his battle plan, McClellan intended for the main attack to be north of Sharpsburg. The Ninth Corps'

role was to "at least to create a diversion in favor of the main attack, with the hope of something more by assailing the enemy's right." While initially limited in scope, the corps' role grew as the battle raged, and its already tough task was hampered by both internal and external factors.

The corps' four divisions fought together for the first time only three days prior at South Mountain. The commanders of all four of those divisions were leading at that level for the first time in this campaign. Changing command structure in the army muddied things further. McClellan suspended the wing structure after South Mountain, relegating Burnside back to corps command. Burnside believed the suspension was only temporary and continued acting as a wing commander, leaving Cox to exercise tactical authority over the corps. This awkward situation did the corps no favors.

The Ninth Corps was the only Federal corps that had to fight to cross Antietam Creek, a stream that was formidable

# Profile: Major General Ambrose Burnside, 1824–81

Born on May 23, 1824, in Indiana, Ambrose Burnside was 19 years old when he received an appointment to the United States Military Academy. He graduated in the Class of 1847. His post-West Point army career was marked mostly by garrison duty, though he was wounded in a fight with the Apaches in 1849. Burnside resigned from the army in 1853 to pursue a manufacturing career. He invented a breech-loading rifle, though it failed to pay off. Falling on hard times, Burnside used his political and personal connections to stay afloat, including his friendship with George B. McClellan. Burnside fought at the battle of First Manassas. President Lincoln gave Burnside command of an expedition to seize the North Carolina coast in 1862, where Burnside performed well. As he brought his forces to Virginia to join the Army of the Potomac, Burnside twice refused command of that army. During the Maryland Campaign, he commanded the army's right wing and oversaw the Ninth Corps' operations during the battle of Antietam. Upon McClellan's removal from army command, Burnside reluctantly assumed the position of commanding general of the Army of the Potomac so that his rival Joseph Hooker did not receive the appointment. Burnside led the army into battle at Fredericksburg on December 13, 1862. It was one of the army's worst defeats. Burnside's "Mud March" tried to restart campaigning around Fredericksburg, but foul weather plagued his plans, which never came to fruition. Lincoln replaced Burnside with Hooker in command of the army shortly thereafter. Burnside's service in the war continued, however. Two months later, he took command of the Department of the Ohio. That fall, he ably defended Knoxville, Tennessee, and prevented it from falling into Confederate hands. Burnside resumed command of the Ninth Corps when it was attached to the Army of the Potomac during the Overland Campaign. The debacle at the battle of the Crater outside of Petersburg, Virginia, on July 30, 1864, ultimately forced him to resign from the army. Burnside spent his postwar years as a businessman, Rhode Island's governor, and a United States Senator until he died on September 13, 1881.

▶ Ambrose Burnside.
(Library of Congress)

enough that it could only be crossed at certain points. A three-arched stone bridge in Burnside's front provided the best access to the Confederate right. But open fields east of the bridge would make any approach difficult and deadly at the hands of enemy soldiers who fortified a 100-foot bluff west of the span.

Those Confederate troops belonged to David R. Jones' division. At the outset of the battle, Jones was not holding Lee's right alone. But the pressure on Lee's left forced the army commander to call John Walker's division to the north. Jones had 2,400 men to cover a three-quarter square mile area that stretched from Cemetery Hill to Snavely's Ford and from Antietam Creek to the Harpers Ferry Road. It stood in front of Boteler's Ford, the army's only route back to Virginia.

Fortunately for Jones' men, they defended some of the toughest terrain of the battlefield. They were positioned to oppose a crossing of the creek, and the climb from the creek to the high ground along the Harpers Ferry Road was an undulating ascent of 180 feet. With Walker's troops gone, Jones only had 500 Georgians, including a smattering of South Carolinians, under Colonel Henry Benning guarding the creek crossings from the Lower Bridge to Snavely's Ford one and a quarter mile downstream. The rest of his division was on the high ground behind Benning's line.

When Burnside received orders to advance, he knew carrying the bridge would be difficult. He learned of a ford about one-half mile below the bridge and determined to not only cross at that bridge

▼ Col. Henry Benning's 400 Georgians had this vantage point of the Lower Bridge from the heights above its western end. They defended the bridge crossing for three hours on September 17. (Author's collection)

but have Brig. Gen. Isaac Rodman take a force of 3,200 men to cross there and unhinge Benning's line. At 10:30 a.m., Rodman's division moved towards the creek to find the crossing.

Upstream at the bridge, Burnside and Cox ordered Col. George Crook's brigade to take the bridge while Colonel Henry Kingsbury's 11th Connecticut provided covering fire. Kingsbury's men advanced into the open floodplain east of the bridge at 10:00 a.m. and were met with a wall of fire from the Georgians. In fifteen minutes, the regiment lost 139 of 440 men, including its colonel who was wounded four times and died the next day. Poor staff and command work derailed Crook's attack. Portions of the brigade ended up 350 yards north of the bridge pinned down by enemy fire.

Rodman likewise ran into problems. The ford earmarked for his command to use was not a suitable military ford. Rodman dispatched skirmishers along the creek bed to move downstream and find another place to cross.

Hearing nothing from Rodman and seeing the failure of the first attack, Burnside and Cox turned to Brig. Gen. Samuel Strugis' division next. Strugis passed the assignment to James Nagle, who selected two regiments numbering 150 men each, the 2nd Maryland and 6th New Hampshire, to dash up Rohrersville Road that ran along the creek's east bank while Nagle's remaining regiments fired from the hill east of the bridge to suppress Benning's fire.

At 11:00 a.m., Nagle's men were in place and they went forward. The two charging

▼ Photos like this cemented the Burnside Bridge as one of America's most recognizable battlefield landmarks. However, this was one of the least deadliest sectors of the Antietam battlefield. Only approximately 600 soldiers fell in the fight for the bridge. (Library of Congress)

regiments received heavy fire as they moved up the roadway and the cover fire was not enough to prevent them from suffering severe casualties that broke up the column before it reached the bridge. A half hour after it began, Nagle's attack fizzled out.

With the fight north of Sharpsburg stalemated, McClellan pressured Burnside even more heavily to carry the bridge. This and the lack of information from Rodman frustrated Burnside. He ordered Sturgis forward again. The task now fell to the 51st New York and 51st Pennsylvania of Colonel Edward Ferrero's brigade. Burnside's artillerymen wheeled 26 guns in close support of the infantry.

Ferrero's 670 men rushed down the hill opposite the eastern end of the bridge at 12:30 p.m. The Georgians' hot and accurate fire greeted these Yankees, who sought cover from the stone and rail fences near the bridge and fired shot after shot into the hillside.

Several factors conspired to make Benning's position untenable. His men had been fighting for close to three hours and were exhausted and low on ammunition. The fire in their front increased once Ferrero's regiments attacked. Lastly, Crook's men found a ford upstream of the bridge while Rodman's column crossed at Snavely's Ford and began marching towards Benning's rear. Sensing the reducing volume of fire from the other side of the creek, Ferrero's men surged across the bridge. At 1:00 p.m., the bridge that forever after bore his name was in Burnside's hands at the cost of 500 Federals and 120 Confederates.

Having seized the bridge, Burnside now had to get his men and artillery over it. Strugis' division was fatigued and needed more ammunition. They secured the bridgehead and linked with Rodman's men but could do no more for the moment. The head of Brig. Gen. Willcox's division crossed

the bridge at 2:00 p.m. to begin deploying astride the Rohrersville Road. Col. Benjamin Christ's brigade deployed north of the road and linked with Col. Thomas Welsh's brigade south of it. Rodman's division continued the line south, with Col. Fairchild's brigade linking the two divisions while Colonel Edward Harland's held the left end of the line. Colonel Hugh Ewing's brigade supported Rodman and Crook's brigade backed up Willcox. Sturgis' division served as a general reserve. By 3:00 p.m., the Ninth Corps' line stretched one mile end to end with 8,000 men immediately ready for the assault.

Burnside's men were not the only Federals west of the creek south of the Sunken Road. At 10:30 a.m., as Richardson's division went into battle, McClellan ordered some of Alfred Pleasonton's cavalry and horse artillery across the Middle Bridge to support Sumner's left. The horsemen drove back a body of Confederate skirmishers along the Boonsboro Pike before the artillery deployed and engaged the enemy guns on Cemetery Hill just in front of Sharpsburg itself.

Confederate riflemen continued to harass Pleasonton's gunners, prompting Fifth Corps division commander George Sykes to send infantry across the bridge and support the artillery. After 2:00 p.m., 1,640 United States Regular infantrymen were west of the creek under Captain Hiram Dryer's command. Dryer's objective was to clear the enemy skirmishers in his front and continue to aid the horse artillery.

By 3:00 p.m., McClellan had control of the five major crossing points of Antietam Creek, and for the first time on September 17, his army held one contiguous line west of the creek. He was now poised to strike the Army of Northern Virginia's right flank. From the Ninth Corps' left to the remnants of the First Corps north of the North

Woods, the line ran 3.5 miles. With the situation on the army's right stabilized but imperfect, McClellan now hoped the Ninth Corps could accomplish "something more by assailing the enemy's right" to crush the enemy and prevent an attack on his army's right flank.

Robert E. Lee was aware of the danger this posed his army, and he also knew how strained his army was at this point in the day. On Cemetery Hill, Brig. Gen. Richard Garnett's and Nathan Evans' brigades eyed the Fifth Corps. Further south, Jenkins', Drayton's, Kemper's, and the remainder of Toombs' brigades held the ridgeline south of the hill. In all, about 2,800 infantry and 28 guns opposed the two Union corps. A. P. Hill appeared from Harpers Ferry and personally reported to Lee at 2:30 p.m. but his division was an hour behind him.

Burnside's advance began at 3:15 p.m. Willcox angled his advance directly at Sharpsburg and Rodman dressed on him, moving the attack in a northwestern direction. Confederate artillery pounded the advancing lines, yet they still moved. The fire and rugged terrain split Willcox's attack as his two brigades had difficulty coordinating their movements. Christ's brigade outpaced Welsh's men. On their right, Captain Charles Poland's Fifth Corps skirmishers stopped short of Cemetery Hill. Portions of Christ's command managed to drive some enemy artillery off Cemetery Hill but the brigade went no further than the Sherrick farm lane.

Welsh's brigade lagged behind Christ because his men had further to advance and more difficult ground to cover. Once these Federals came onto the firing line, they encountered Jenkins' brigade in and around a stone mill. Two Massachusetts guns arrived to support the advance. Jenkins' men were only driven out of their

▼ This view shows the Fifth Corps' field of advance from the Confederate position at the top of Cemetery Hill. Federal artillery deployed on the ridge in the middle of the picture while Sykes' United States Regulars advanced towards the camera on both sides of the Boonsboro Pike, seen here running between the power lines. (Author's collection)

position after a close-quarters fight. Some of Welsh's men pursued the Confederates into the boundary street of Sharpsburg.

Fairchild's New Yorkers went in on Rodman's left. Artillery fire and deep ravines plagued their advance. At the top of the rise where Jones' main battle line lay, Kemper's and Drayton's men—about 590 total—waited for the New Yorkers to close within 50 yards before loosing a volley from behind a stone wall. The Federals shouldered their own guns and exchanged fire. Soon, officers of the 9th New York grabbed the regiment's colors and yelled for their men to charge and break the stalemate. Bayonets and clubbed muskets were used in the intense melee. Fairchild's men drove the enemy from the field and, along with Welsh pursued them into Sharpsburg's streets. The New York brigade lost 48 percent of the 940 men it carried into combat.

Harland's brigade had a tougher advance. Terrain, bungled orders, and the advance of Fairchild's brigade carried Harland's right regiment, the 8th Connecticut, far in advance of the brigade's two other regiments, creating a half-mile gap in the Ninth Corps' line. Rodman rode back to bring up the two rear regiments—the green 16th Connecticut and 4th Rhode Island—and was shot down in the process. Those two regiments saw Confederate battle lines advancing towards them and moved into the Sherrick cornfield to oppose the enemy.

At the peak of the Ninth Corps' attack, the Fifth Corps also found limited success at the base of Cemetery Hill. The Union skirmishers south of the Boonsboro Pike reached the Sherrick farm lane while Dryer's men north of the road advanced beyond. Their advance cleared Cemetery Hill of Confederate forces, and Dryer wanted to push on. His skirmishers north

of the road reached just below the northern crest of the hill.

Robert E. Lee himself rode into the crisis, scrounging portions of various commands and sending them towards Cemetery Hill, telling them, "Go in cheerfully boys." Simultaneously, he shuffled artillery batteries south of town to form along the Harpers Ferry Road. He managed to scrape together enough batteries from all across the field that by the end of the day, 43 pieces clustered to protect the Confederate right.

Lee also received timely help in the form of A. P. Hill's division. Hill's men had left Harpers Ferry at 7:30 that morning. Following a march of 15 miles in nine hours, they arrived in time to bolster Lee's crumbling line.

Maxcy Gregg's South Carolinians struck first. With the sun at their backs, they advanced downhill to the edge of the

▲ Known for his aggressive nature in battle, Maj. Gen. A. P. Hill showed glimpses of promise but continually clashed with his commanding general "Stonewall" Jackson. Hill was placed under arrest by Jackson earlier in the campaign but was allowed to return to command by Harpers Ferry. (Library of Congress)

Sherrick cornfield and hit Harland's two New England regiments there. Two South Carolina regiments hurdled the stone fence on the west edge of the cornfield and attacked the 16th Connecticut (which had been in the army less than a month) and the 4th Rhode Island. The shaky Union regiments repulsed Gregg's men twice. Gregg threw a third regiment into the fight and tipped the balance in favor of his men, who forced the Connecticut and Rhode Island men from the field.

Hill's arrival did not meet with initial success everywhere. Captain David McIntosh's battery, the first of Hill's units to arrive, deployed east of

◀ A Congressman and lawyer before the Civil War, Brigadier General Lawrence O'Bryan Branch also held the distinction of finishing first in his class at Princeton in 1838. Branch started the war as a private and then rose to brigadier general in Hill's division. He was mortally wounded, supposedly by the same bullet that wounded Maxcy Gregg, during the later stages of the battle of Antietam. (Library of Congress)

▼ Guns marking the position of Captain William Pegram's Purcell Artillery sit along the Harpers Ferry Road overlooking the attack fields of Rodman's Union division and A. P. Hill's Confederate division. (Author's collection)

Harpers Ferry Road and came under attack from the 8th Connecticut and suffered from Federal artillery fire that accompanied the Ninth Corps' advance. These dual factors forced McIntosh to abandon his guns briefly. Toombs' brigade reoccupied the guns before the Federals got their hands on them.

Brigadier General Lawrence Branch's North Carolina brigade arrived next in Hill's column. It moved north toward the exposed flank of the 8th Connecticut and open gap in the Ninth Corps' line. One by one, the Union regiments along the Harpers Ferry Road ridge peeled back under this pressure.

Branch's and Toombs' brigades, joined by that of Maryland native James Archer, now drove down the slope to press their attack. Two regiments of Col. Ewing's brigade momentarily stopped them on the west edge of the cornfield. Gregg's men went back into the fight against Ewing's left and rear and forced his men back, too. The Confederates attempted to advance further, but the deployment of Strugis' division in reserve quelled that effort.

From his vantage, Cox saw that the strength currently at his disposal could not crush the enemy right. No support came, and Cox ordered the corps back to the heights west of the Lower Bridge.

▲ Previous spread: Besides their own wounded, Union doctors had to care for approximately 2,500 Confederate sick and wounded who were left behind. Army of the Potomac Medical Director Jonathan Letterman believed his surgeons cared for the wounded enemy as best they could, for "Humanity teaches us that a wounded and prostrate foe is not then our enemy." (Library of Congress)

▶ The Maryland Campaign was the last major campaign in which Fitz John Porter commanded troops. He was relieved of command in November and was found guilty in a court-martial case in January 1863 for multiple charges leveled at him by Maj. Gen. John Pope during the Second Manassas Campaign. Porter's name was cleared and his army rank restored in 1886. (Library of Congress)

## Letterman Plan

The battles of the Maryland Campaign left approximately 21,000 wounded soldiers to be mended. Removing the wounded to hospitals in a timely manner to increase their chances of survival was a Herculean task for the medical departments of both armies. Antietam was the first battle where Jonathan Letterman, the Army of the Potomac's Medical Director, implemented a new plan to more readily and properly care for wounded soldiers. Letterman's plan standardized the evacuation of wounded from the battlefield by administering a triage system that categorized wounded soldiers and dictated who was treated first. He also ensured that medical supplies were effectively distributed. This system, called the Letterman Plan, is still the basis for the United States Army's medical procedures today.

The Ninth Corps' withdrawal affected the fight at the Middle Bridge. Dryer's left was unprotected as the Ninth Corps fell back. Besides, Dryer's proposed advance never came to fruition as it exceeded his orders, which were to support artillery. His men pulled back, too. Porter's corps—which had fewer than 4,000 men available for action—was dispersed to support both ends of the Army of the Potomac at this point.

The action south and east of Sharpsburg produced another 3,600 casualties—about 350 at the Middle Bridge and approximately 3,200 during the Ninth Corps' attack. After twelve hours of fighting, nearly 23,000 soldiers of both armies were casualties: one soldier every two seconds.

Lee's army had 38,000 men present on the field and lost roughly 10,500 men, 27 percent of his army. Three of Lee's nine

▶ The Burnside Bridge, originally known as the Rohrbach or Lower Bridge, was built in 1836 at the cost of $3,200. Cars used the bridge until 1966. Today, many people visit Antietam to walk across this historic span. (Author's collection)

infantry division commanders went down during the battle, and the officer corps down to regimental command was equally in bad shape. Fifty-one percent of the regimental commanders at the beginning of the battle were casualties.

The Army of the Potomac was also hit hard on September 17. McClellan commanded 70,000 men total that day, 12,500 of whom, or 18 percent, became casualties, including two of his six corps commanders. The army's regimental command structure changed because of the officer casualties on the battlefield—38 percent of the regiments were commanded by someone different at the end of the battle compared to its start.

Nonetheless, the battle was a Union victory. Though only slight gains were made, Lee no longer had a barrier between himself and the Federal army. The five major Antietam Creek crossings were in Federal hands. McClellan could now bring the full weight of his strength against Lee's line. The Confederates were caught between the Federal army and the Potomac River.

The setting sun silenced Antietam's guns and darkened the shattered landscape. Lanterns bobbed across the farms and woodlots of Sharpsburg in search of wounded souls. Fatigued men caught their collective breath around campfires and waited to see what tomorrow might bring. America's bloodiest single day was over.

# The Campaign Ends

The battle of Antietam was not the conclusion of the Maryland Campaign. Both army commanders had plans to continue the campaign to achieve their goals. That required Lee to move his army from Maryland back into Virginia. McClellan pursued and the last battle of the campaign was fought along the Potomac River at Shepherdstown on September 19–20, 1862.

▼ Robert E. Lee's headquarters stood in a tent in an oak grove west of Sharpsburg. This area likewise served as a staging area for Confederate troops arriving from Harpers Ferry before being put into the battle line on the other side of town. (Author's collection)

One by one, the tired, powder-grimed generals of the Army of Northern Virginia made their way to army headquarters west of Sharpsburg. These officers had just led their men through a trying day, one of the bloodiest for the army but one of its best-fought in the war. They reported to Lee the status of their commands. After listening to all but consulting with none, Lee told his subordinates to "strengthen your forces" to prepare to fight again at Sharpsburg on September 18.

HEADQUARTERS SITE GEN. R. E. LEE

Across Antietam Creek, George B. McClellan laid plans for an attack by William Franklin's Sixth Corps on Lee's left the next day. He called on reinforcements in the form of Pennsylvania militia and divisions under Maj. Gen. Darius Couch and Brigadier General Andrew Humphreys to join him at the battlefield.

The next day, daylight revealed the catastrophe of September 17. McClellan delayed Franklin's attack until the expected reinforcements reached the field to make the offensive "a certain thing." When those commands did reach the field (except the militia who refused to leave Pennsylvania), all-night marches sapped their offensive potential. Additionally, McClellan awaited 38 tons of ammunition for his long-range artillery. Citing these complications, he pushed off any attack until September 19.

Lee, too, sought to renew the battle north of Sharpsburg against the enemy's right, but his subordinates did not believe any such attempt would succeed. Upon reporting this judgment, Stephen Lee saw "a shade come over General Lee's face." With his physical barrier between his army and the enemy's shattered—the Federals now held all five crossings of Antietam Creek—and no chance for offensive success, Lee prepared his army to return to Virginia. Retreating under the cover of night, the army was safely across the Potomac River by the morning of September 19.

The recrossing of the river was not an abandonment of the campaign for Lee. Instead, with the river between him and McClellan, Lee ordered his cavalry to ride north and secure a bridgehead at Williamsport, Maryland, 28 miles up the curvy river from the army's crossing point at Boteler's Ford near Shepherdstown. The rest of the Army of Northern Virginia would follow. If all went according to plan, Lee's army would be back in Maryland after stealing a march on their adversaries and

▼ Called Boteler's Ford, Blackford's Ford, or Packhorse Ford, this river crossing served the region since the early 1700s. Competing with the Blackford ferry upriver near Shepherdstown and then a new covered bridge in 1850, the ford's traffic consisted of more locals than travelers. (Author's collection)

the prospect of winning a battle north of that river could again be realized.

While the majority of the army marched towards Williamsport, Lee left a rear guard at Boteler's Ford under his artillery chief, Brig. Gen. William Pendleton. Two battered infantry brigades (600 men), one of cavalry, and 44 guns protected the army's rear. Lee did not expect much of a Federal pursuit.

But when McClellan and his subordinates discovered the disappearance of the enemy,

◄ William Nelson Pendleton graduated from West Point in 1830 but spent most of the three decades prior to the Civil War as a clergyman. Many of the men and officers in the Army of Northern Virginia lost faith in Pendleton by September 1862, yet he retained his position as the army's chief of artillery throughout the war. (Library of Congress)

▼ Ferry Hill was the home of "Stonewall" Jackson staffer Henry Kyd Douglas. During the battle of Shepherdstown, Union cannon crowned the hill and engaged in a long-range artillery duel with Confederate guns guarding the river crossing. (Library of Congress)

Pleasonton's cavalry quickly pursued towards Boteler's Ford. Pendleton's artillerymen announced their presence, prompting a duel across the river. McClellan ordered the Sixth Corps to the ford to aid Pleasonton. He soon replaced them with Porter's Fifth Corps once he learned of Stuart's successful incursion at Williamsport and prepared to send Franklin in that direction.

Porter's orders were to not cross the river unless he saw a chance to damage the enemy without inflicting any harm to his own command. Porter lined the north bank of the river with infantry while more artillery arrived. Near sunset, he saw a favorable chance to hurt Lee's rear guard. Union infantry stormed across the river and scattered Pendleton's command.

Pendleton's subordinates extracted most of the guns from Porter's clutches, leaving only four in the Federals' hands. In his haste to leave the scene, Pendleton assumed he lost all the rear guard's guns.

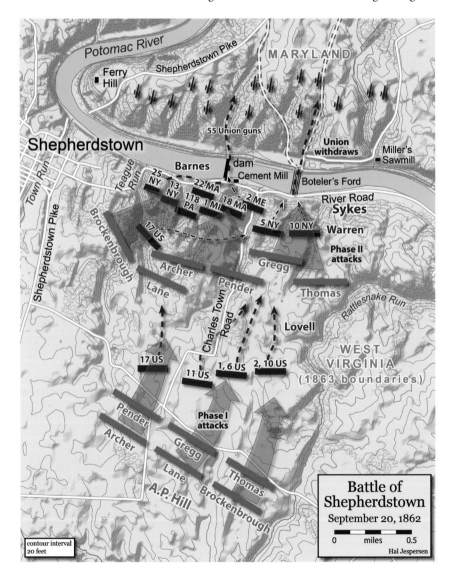

Battle of Shepherdstown
September 20, 1862

0    miles    0.5

Hal Jespersen

contour interval 20 feet

An exasperated Pendleton rode throughout the night seeking help before reporting the situation to Lee personally after midnight. This development shocked Lee, who quickly ordered most of his army to cease its march towards Williamsport and return to Shepherdstown to manage the threat in his rear.

Porter was encouraged by the success of September 19 and, with McClellan's blessing, ordered a reconnaissance across the river scheduled for the morning of September 20 under Sykes' command. A miscue in orders made Pleasonton's accompanying cavalry late; Sykes' infantry advanced south from the river alone.

▶ George Sykes commanded the division composed of all of the United States Regular infantry in the Eastern Theater. Nicknamed "Tardy George," a moniker dating back to his West Point days and not necessarily reflective of his battlefield performance, Sykes rose to corps command before Gettysburg but in 1864 was transferred to the Trans-Mississippi for the rest of the war. (Library of Congress)

Less than a mile south of the ford, Sykes' vanguard ran into the head of Lee's army, A. P. Hill's division. Hill's men deployed into line and pushed Sykes' men back to the cliffs overlooking the river. Sykes recognized this was no position to fight in and ordered his entire force to cross back into Maryland under the cover of 55 guns. One green regiment, the 118th Pennsylvania, remained behind following a misunderstanding of orders and faced Hill's division alone. Hill's veterans cut the Pennsylvania ranks to pieces. After driving Sykes' men across the river, Hill's men remained on the river's south shore to guarantee the safety of Lee's rear. Casualties totaled over 600 men between the two sides.

Once night fell, Lee resumed his army's march to Williamsport. Doing so made Lee starkly realize the condition of his army, and it was not a good one. This recognition, along with news that Stuart's bridgehead at Williamsport had been collapsed by Federal troops on the night of September 20, forced Lee to abandon another movement into Maryland. "The condition of our troops now demanded repose," Lee conceded, and his hope of victory north of the Potomac River in September 1862 was never realized.

The battle of Shepherdstown demonstrated to McClellan that Lee's army was still

dangerous. His army, like Lee's, was worn down by the previous months of campaigning and fighting. Believing he achieved his goal of rescuing Maryland and driving Lee back to Virginia, McClellan settled his army north of the river. The 18-day-long Maryland Campaign was over.

▲ Dedicated in 1880 in the center of Antietam National Cemetery, the Private Soldier Monument stands guard over the graves of 4,776 Union soldiers. He faces north with a simple inscription beneath his feet: "Not for themselves, but for their country." (Library of Congress)

# Afterword

The repulse of the first Confederate campaign north of the Potomac River prompted President Abraham Lincoln to issue a war-changing measure, the Emancipation Proclamation. Antietam's impact reached far beyond the battlegrounds of Maryland and Virginia in September 1862.

Messengers raced from the State Department on the morning of September 22, 1862. To all the Federal offices they went with a notice in hand for the heads of those departments to convene at noon in the President's office.

The meeting began without much flourish as the Cabinet discussed general matters and listened to President Lincoln read a chapter from Artemus Ward, a humorist. Then, the President "took a graver tone," wrote Secretary of the Treasury Salmon Chase.

Lincoln reminded his cabinet of the Preliminary Emancipation Proclamation he showed them two months ago. He admitted his thoughts "about the relation of this war to Slavery" consumed him. He told them now was the time to announce this war-changing measure to the country. "I wish it were a better time. I wish we were in a better condition," he admitted. When he learned of the Confederate invasion of Maryland, Lincoln made a promise that "as soon as it should be driven out of Maryland, to issue a Proclamation of Emancipation,"

◀ Despite a shaky hand from greeting hundreds of visitors, Abraham Lincoln signed the Emancipation Proclamation into effect on New Year's Day 1863. "I never, in my life, felt more certain that I was doing right, than I do in signing this paper," he told onlookers to the momentous event. (Library of Congress)

the President said. "The rebel army is now driven out, and I am going to fulfill that promise." Word of Lincoln's proclamation reached the country the next day.

Antietam's carnage will always be tied to Lincoln's Emancipation Proclamation. It was, after all, the event Lincoln needed to issue it. The preliminary document gave the Confederate states 100 days to rejoin the Union. If they did not, Lincoln and the United States Army would free the slaves held in bondage in territory occupied by the Confederacy. After Antietam, the nation would never be as it once was, half slave and half free. It would either be two nations split by the institution of slavery or one nation without that institution.

September 1862 was the best chance the Confederacy had to achieve its independence. Confederate armies advanced north from the Potomac River to the Mississippi River. None of those attempts succeeded. Lee's movement

into Maryland was the first of those to be turned back. Interest from Great Britain and France to support the Confederacy dropped off after the Maryland Campaign. Marylanders did not rise in large numbers to carry their state into the Confederacy. Lincoln's Republican Party did sustain some losses in the 1862 midterm elections but still maintained a majority in both houses of Congress, 16 of 18 state governorships, and all but three state legislatures, far from what was needed for political opposition to stop the Union war effort.

Robert E. Lee's failure to win a battlefield victory north of the Potomac River in the summer of 1862 meant there would be more battlefields where the fate of these two combatants would be decided. None of those battles stacked up to Antietam in terms of the ramifications from their results. This single day of unequaled bloodshed changed American lives forever.

▲ President Abraham Lincoln visited the Army of the Potomac in the vicinity of the battlefield for four days in October 1862. He met with commanding general George McClellan, reviewed the army, and toured the battlefield. Alexander Gardner captured this scene on October 3 in front of the Grove house, whose roof can be seen in the background, on the west end of Sharpsburg. Lincoln reviewed the Union Fifth Corps here and visited with the wounded of both sides. Inside the house, Lincoln "remarked to the wounded Confederates that if they had no objection he would be pleased to take them by the hand." (Library of Congress)

▲ The Emancipation Proclamation has appeared in many different forms since Lincoln signed it into law. This popularized and artistic version dates from 1888. (Library of Congress)

# Further Reading

Carman, Ezra A. *The Maryland Campaign of September 1862*. Edited by Thomas G. Clemens. 3 volumes. El Dorado Hills, CA: Savas Beatie, 2010, 2012, 2017.

Gallagher, Gary W., ed. *The Antietam Campaign*. Chapel Hill, NC: University of North Carolina Press, 1999.

Gottfried, Bradley M. *The Maps of Antietam*. El Dorado Hills, CA: Savas Beatie, 2012.

Harsh, Joseph L. *Taken at the Flood: Robert E. Lee & Confederate Strategy in the Maryland Campaign of 1862*. Kent, OH: Kent State University Press, 1999.

Hartwig, D. Scott. *To Antietam Creek: The Maryland Campaign of September 1862*. Baltimore, MD: Johns Hopkins University Press, 2012.

Hoptak, John David. *The Battle of South Mountain*. Charleston, SC: The History Press, 2011.

McPherson, James M. *Antietam: Crossroads of Freedom*. New York: Oxford University Press, 2002.

Murfin, James V. *The Gleam of Bayonets: The Battle of Antietam and the Maryland Campaign of 1862*. New York: Thomas Yoseloff, 1965.

Orrison, Robert and Kevin R. Pawlak. *To Hazard All: A Guide to the Maryland Campaign, 1862*. El Dorado Hills, CA: Savas Beatie, 2018.

Rafuse, Ethan S. *Antietam, South Mountain, & Harpers Ferry: A Battlefield Guide*. Lincoln, NE: University of Nebraska Press, 2008.

Rafuse, Ethan S. *McClellan's War: The Failure of Moderation in the Struggle for the Union*. Bloomington, IN: Indiana University Press, 2005.

Reardon, Carol and Tom Vossler. *A Field Guide to Antietam*. Chapel Hill, NC: University of North Carolina Press, 2016.

Sears, Stephen W. *Landscape Turned Red: The Battle of Antietam*. Boston, MA: Houghton Mifflin, 2003.

Vermilya, Daniel J. *That Field of Blood: The Battle of Antietam, September 17, 1862*. El Dorado Hills, CA: Savas Beatie, 2018.

# Acknowledgements

Many people helped make this book possible. First, I want to thank Ted Savas, who first pitched this idea to me, and the folks at Casemate Publishers for making this an enjoyable project. Many eyes read early drafts of the manuscript and made useful comments. Thanks especially to Jay Ferris, Michael Hill, Bill Sagle, Matt Borders, Jim Buchanan, and Phill Greenwalt, and also to Hal Jespersen who graciously adapted the maps for this book. To my many Antietam colleagues, this manuscript has benefitted from our constant discussions and sharing of knowledge. Lastly, thanks to my family for allowing me to pursue my passion and share it with others.

▼ Sunrise over the Miller cornfield on September 17, 2012. (Author's collection)

# Index